Effective

SELF HYPNOSIS

Pathways to the Unconscious

C. Alexander Simpkins Ph.D.

&

Annellen M. Simpkins Ph.D.

Radiant Dolphin Press

Library of Congress Control Number
00-090483

ISBN 0-9679113-0-3
ISBN (with cassette) 0-9679113-1-1

Radiant Dolphin Press
San Diego, California

Printed in the United States of America

First Edition
06 05 04 03 02 01   3 5 7 9 10 8 6 4 2

Cover Art by Carmen Z. Simpkins

Carmen Z. Simpkins' abstract expressionist paintings suggest mood, movement, and mysticism. Simpkins has been painting for 75 years. Her first solo show took place in Camden, Maine, in 1962 at the Broadlawn Gallery. She has exhibited throughout the world, and her works are in private collections in Europe and the Americas. Her works can be seen in her galleries in Clinton, South Carolina and Sebastian, Florida.

⌘

We Dedicate This Book to:

Our parents, Carmen and Nat Simpkins
and Naomi and Herb Minkin,
Our children, Alura and Alex,
for their patience, forbearance, and willingness to experiment
confidently with the techniques,
And our clients, past, present, and future, may they always
continue to grow.

⌘

Acknowledgment

We thank our hypnosis teachers
Milton H. Erickson, G. Wilson Shaffer, and Ernest Rossi
for sharing their great wisdom and clinical acumen.
We are grateful to Elizabeth Erickson
for her corrections, advice, and support.
Any errors, limitations or omissions are our own.

Contents

Foreword
by
Ernest L. Rossi Ph.D.

This book is organized around three well thought-out steps: theory is developed as the background throughout; exercises make the theory real; and finally, clear directions are given for specific clinical applications.

Not only do the authors give a complete and well developed history of hypnosis with an emphasis on self hypnosis, but they show how particular practices evolve out of different frames of reference.

Then, going on to my favorite area, the authors achieve a uniquely balanced integration in their presentation of direct and indirect suggestion. They do not make the mistake of thinking of indirect suggestion as a way of prevaricating in the therapeutic situation. Rather, indirect suggestions are used in the correct sense, the Ericksonian sense, of bypassing the ego's learned limitations and accessing inner resources. Even when these new resources are not fully available for clients, they can learn to access them themselves. This becomes the core of what therapeutic trance is and remains faithful to the core creative essence of Erickson's thought. Instead of the classical misconception of mistaking suggestion for hypnosis, the therapeutic trance is a way of enhancing the client's sensitivity to the mind-body system. Once again, they are correcting another misconception, following the Ericksonian idea of hypnosis as sensitivity to one's unconscious rather than simply suggestion.

Their work gains an extra dimension of reality through their use of exercises throughout the text. For every bit of theory they introduce an exercise to illustrate. For example, the different forms of suggestion are illustrated with exercises. Sensory awareness exercises follow theory of mind-body interactions. Hand levitation and warming or cooling are examples of kinesthetic alterations. Exercises in inner imagery illustrate visual effects. Instruction in time distortion teaches other hallucinatory experiences.

Finally, the authors present ways to apply the techniques developed in the book to common applications. They consistently use the therapeutic trance as the primary source for learning.

An unusually lucid presentation and integration!

Introduction

Truth refines but does not obscure
--Nathaniel Stone Simpkins, 1836

There are many books written about hypnosis, but self hypnosis is unique, requiring special skills. The individual attempting self hypnosis must be both the hypnotist and the subject simultaneously. The dilemma in self hypnosis is how to voluntarily do the involuntary, to deliberately be spontaneous and regain rapport with your own inner self.

Self hypnosis returns you to balance. Both the conscious and unconscious can learn to work together for orienting and problem solving in hypnotic work. We conducted a research project investigating whether therapy that attempts to make the unconscious become conscious is more effective than hypnotherapy that develops the unconscious and without making it conscious. Generally, both methods tended to be effective. (Simpkins & Simpkins, 1983) leading to our subsequent inclusion of both conscious and unconscious in self hypnosis. You will learn to return to natural functioning with your unconscious and to cooperate with your inner needs in a healthy and positive way.

Individual differences can be taken into account when you learn about your own inner sensitivities, abilities, and needs. As abilities unfold, you develop openness to creative therapeutic process and thereby tap a positive reservoir of potential from within. By recognizing the possibility that you can have capacities beyond what you know consciously, better adaptations to problems and difficulties can emerge.

Self hypnosis facilitates constructive responses and better use of potentials. Normally, we have routine patterns of thoughts, attitudes, concerns, and feelings. Like a television set receiving only three channels, this becomes the limited spectrum of possibility for television viewing. We tune the television to these channels only, ignoring any other signals. Then, one day we become curious about new possibilities for input and decide to put a satellite dish on the roof. Suddenly new channels become available with new programming options. Similarly, our assumptions limit us to a certain range of experiences. Other mental events are either disregarded or experienced as meaningless static. Openness to the unconscious through hypnosis draws in more data and new perspectives. These new potentials may be integrated to expand the horizons of experience.

People vary on how they respond to hypnosis. For those comfortable with suggestion, hypnosis will seem to affect them through the heightened suggestibility they discover. Some people will feel things develop in their bodies from merely an imagined thought. For them, hypnosis is experienced in ideomotor phenomena. They may watch in amazement as their hand raises, seemingly all by itself. Others, who are naturally comfortable with trance, may feel as if they fall deeply asleep and remember nothing. Once you become familiar with your own personal response to hypnosis, you can broaden and evolve to learn other responses. Trance and suggestion need not be separate: they are One.

Rather than programming your mind with direct suggestion, the traditional stereotype of hypnosis, this book teaches you how to sensitize to intuitions from your unconscious processes. Paradoxically, this may result in desensitization to learned limitations, as will be shown later. Spontaneous responses occur, rather than redundant conditioning. Throughout we invite you to interact with your responses and use them creatively.

About This Book

Self hypnosis is an art of inner communication that can be used for many purposes. This book is written for professionals who are interested in helping themselves or their clients, using some hypnotic facilitation, and for the person who is interested in developing skills in self hypnosis to bring about changes. We recognize that professionals are accustomed to a complex lexicon, but wherever possible, we have used simpler terminology so that the intelligent layman can understand. Although the exercises are directed to the person performing the exercise, therapists can use the exercises themselves or adapt them for clients.

This book is divided into four parts. Part I, The Story of Hypnosis, shows the evolution and expansion of self hypnosis, growing out of the traditions of hypnosis itself. Included are early developments and clinical applications along with later research findings.

Part II, The Pillars of Hypnosis, explains the fundamental tools used in hypnosis: the unconscious mind, the mind and body working together, and suggestion. Exercises are also offered, so you can develop the skills used in self hypnosis.

Part III, Pathways to Trance, gives step-by-step instructions for inducing hypnosis in yourself. Find your way into trance by trying varied self hypnotic experiences. We encourage you to experiment with many kinds of exercises. These are opportunities to try out new skills. Special work with resistances can help people who find it difficult to develop a trance or respond to self suggestion.

Part IV, Navigating the Sea of Life, offers approaches to specific problems, using and developing the self hypnotic skills taught earlier in the book. Self hypnosis can be a practical tool for specific target areas while also facilitating a general constructive process within. These applications can also be viewed as paradigms for more generalized personal development.

How to Use This Book

In using this book, you may not want to start at the beginning with the historical and theoretical sections. Hypnosis is first and foremost an experience. Some might prefer to experience it first, going directly to the exercises, and then learn about the theory of hypnosis later. Others might find that they want to understand the theory and history first, to experiment later with practical exercises from a firm theoretical orientation, a map for the journey. Both ways can work, and probably, most people will do both in time.

The book encourages you to experiment with exercises throughout. Many of the exercises have complex instructions that might seem difficult to remember. You will achieve the greatest success by reading through each exercise you want to try at least twice. Then set the book aside, find a comfortable, quiet place to sit or lie down, and try to do the exercise. Since these exercises are mostly directed toward unconscious response, you do not need to remember every instruction. The unconscious tends to find its own way when given the opportunity. Repeat an exercise over a span of time for maximum results. Trance instructions in earlier chapters should be practiced thoroughly to develop skills with self hypnosis before attempting the applications in Part IV.

Exercises are intended to have wider applications than their specific suggestions. Be creative and adapt them to your own resources, interests, and talents. Many people are independent individuals who want to work things out on their own. In the context of these experiments they can discover techniques and ways of helping themselves. However, some problems require the expertise of a professional, or some people do better with the guidance of a hypnotist or psychotherapist.

We believe that psychotherapists can learn the hypnotic perspective best from experiencing it themselves. Self hypnosis is an excellent way to become more open to the hypnotic use of the unconscious. Erickson showed us the vast positive potential of the unconscious. Reactions to the exercises should be felt and thought about. We hope you will be able to find your own positive potential for growth and development through the use of this book.

PART ONE

The Story of Hypnosis

The hypnotic effect always takes place within the person who is being hypnotized. The hypnotist may facilitate the process, but ultimately, it is an inner experience. Hypnosis can now be viewed as a form of self hypnosis. But the idea of self hypnosis as something that a person could do without a hypnotist was not discovered until much later in the history of hypnosis. We discover the inner thread of self hypnosis hidden within the tapestry of the history of hypnosis itself.

One

Early History

Returning to the root
We get the essence

--Zen saying

ypnotic phenomena have been known for centuries. The ancient Egyptians viewed these states as mystical highly effective methods of therapy. The famous Ebers papyrus, dated about 3000 BC, described procedures identical to modern hypnosis. Hypnotism originated from magic much the same way that chemistry arose from alchemy and astronomy came from astrology.

Janet's (1925) monumental study of psychotherapy *Psychological Healing* included a comprehensive review of hypnosis through the ages, tracing back the use of hypnosis for many centuries. The basic concepts of hypnosis were understood and described even before hypnosis was isolated as a discipline of its own. Janet believed that the study of what would later be called suggestion was the foundation of psychology.

Hypnotic phenomena were used at times throughout history, but it was not until the eighteenth century in Europe that hypnosis would be studied and practiced extensively.

Two Approaches to Hypnosis

Two main branches of hypnosis developed in Europe simultaneously, mesmerism and somnambulism. Mesmerists believed that the phenomena results from a magnetic force, harnessed and used by the hypnotist. The second perspective, at first called somnambulism, later renamed hypnosis, viewed the phenomena as emerging from an inner experience within the subject. Both forms have continued to live on, with charismatic proponents and theories. Modern views blend them together.

Mesmerism

Franz Anton Mesmer (1734-1815) was a major popularizer of animal magnetism, later known as mesmerism. He drew his ideas from several earlier theorists. Paracelsus (1493-1541), a physician and mystic, speculated that the human body was under the influence of the stars, acting like a magnet. Van Helmont (1577-1644) introduced the idea of animal magnetism. He believed that a magnetic fluid emanating from human beings could be influenced by the will.

Mesmer developed these ideas further and put them into practice, with many dramatic cures. He was controversial and theatrical. His pamphlets portrayed him as a dedicated man who arrived in Paris with a discovery that would put an end to human suffering. He appealed to the leading French academic and scientific organizations for support and recognition of his work, but he never received it.

Mesmer's medical dissertation (1766) was written on the influence of the planets on human beings. He believed a mutual influence exists between the heavenly bodies and the human body. The interaction alternates between an ebb and a flow of a magnetic-like fluid that affects the nervous system.

This property of the animal body which brings it under the influence of the heavenly bodies and the reciprocal action of those surrounding it, as shown by its analogy with the Magnet, induced me to term it Animal Magnetism. (Mesmer, in Tinterow 1970, 55)

People were healthy when the fluid flowed freely, reminiscent of the Chinese concept of internal energy, *chi*, important for health. Disease resulted from blockage and improper balance.

Individuals could control and reinforce the fluid's action by "mesmerizing" or massaging the body's "poles" and thereby overcoming the obstacle, inducing a "crisis" often in the form of convulsions, and restoring health or "harmony" of man with nature. (Darnton 1970, 4)

Many were convinced that Mesmer held the key to a tremendous power because he was able to create such visible results, sending his patients into convulsions. Mesmer and his followers emphasized the great influence a magnetizer had on the subject. This influence depended on the hypnotic rapport between subject and magnetizer.

One of Mesmer's distinguished disciples, Marquis de Puységur, observed three central features in mesmerism. First, the subject could only hear what the mesmerist said and was oblivious to all else. Second, the subject accepted suggestions uncritically. Third, the subject recalled nothing of trance when awake. This interpretation of Mesmer's theory implied that the patient was the passive recipient of the active effects. Some modern conceptions about hypnosis derive from such views.

Mesmer was unsuccessful in gaining medical acceptance for mesmerism. The Royal Society of Medicine, the influential medical group of the period, formed a commission that included the American expert on electricity, Benjamin Franklin, to hear Mesmer's claims. They judged animal magnetism did not exist and that the cures Mesmer claimed were due to suggestion and imagination.

Mesmer and his followers appealed to the masses with pamphlets claiming that the privileged classes were trying to suppress Mesmer's attempts to help the common man. The government became alarmed, and tried to restrict Mesmer. Mesmer left France, to live in Switzerland. The outbreak of the French Revolution dominated public concern, and thus most investigations of magnetism in France stopped. However, though temporarily restrained, mesmeric currents seethed beneath the surface of the times, to be released again later.

Somnambulism

Despite Mesmer's failure to gain approval from the scientific community, interest in the phenomenon was not lost. In the early 1800's several Frenchmen again began to work with it. These pioneering men quietly experimented in their own homes and offices. Details of their lives as persons are lost in obscure descriptions of forgotten memories, retained only in the pages of rare books. But these unknown explorers gave us theories that became basic and background to modern hypnosis. They considered hypnosis to be a form of sleep. They called it somnambulism.

Bertrand (1820) was one of the first to state that somnambulism was due solely to the workings of the imagination. He believed that suggestion was the determiner of the state, not fluids or magnets. In his book, *Traite du Somnambulism*, Bertrand described the movements, actions, and hallucinations that could be aroused in the mind of the subject.

Deleuze (1825) discussed anesthesias, amnesias, and posthypnotic phenomena, some of the characteristic applications of hypnosis used today.

The Abbé Faria, a notable cleric, induced somnambulism by dynamic command, simply saying to patients, "I wish you to go to sleep." He used somnambulism with dramatic success for the benefit of many people. He is credited as the founder of the technique of rapid induction, commonly used by skilled practitioners today. The use of hypnosis became the focus.

Noizêt, a friend of Bertrand, wrote a book that linked Bertrand with the doctrine that later became basic to the Nancy School. He stated:

The fundamental psychological law which is at work is the law in accordance with which every idea tends to become an action; the suggested action is performed because the idea of the action has made its way into the subject's consciousness. (Janet 1925, 157)

The foundation of modern artificial somnambulism could now be viewed as a normal state, working with the general laws of imagination, expectant attention, and desire. Modern developments in the art and science of hypnosis and hypnotherapy were in place. Self hypnosis incorporates many concepts from this orientation.

The Beginnings of Self Hypnosis

James Braid (1795-1860) is credited with giving the name "Hypnotism" to differentiate the phenomenon from mesmerism. Concurrent with the French somnambulists, Braid was working with hypnosis in Manchester, England. He was a conservative surgeon who carefully experimented and wrote, seeking always to give scientific meaning to his findings. Braid helped hypnosis gain acceptance.

Braid initially believed that sensory fixation of the eyelids was central to trance induction. Rolling the eyes upwards caused a paralysis of the eye muscles, leading to the phenomenon of hypnosis. Braid stated:

> *It is this very principle, of over-exerting the attention by keeping it riveted to one subject or idea which is not of itself of an exciting nature, and over exercising one set of muscles, and the state of the strained eyes, with the suppressed respiration, and general repose, which attend such experiments, which excites in the brain and whole nervous system that peculiar state which I call hypnotism, or nervous sleep. (Braid 1960, 30)*

Braid produced trance in his family and friends by having their eyeballs fixed in the same position and their minds riveted to one idea of an object held above their eyes. Eventually their eyes closed with a vibratory motion as they entered an altered state. At this point, Braid could raise his subject's arm or leg and the subject would remain in this position. This is called catalepsy. Following this phase, Braid saw a deeply relaxed, refreshing sleep with no rigidity of the muscles. These observations proved to him that he had discovered a phenomenon different from mesmerism.

Braid's earlier theory of hypnosis emphasized the importance of sensory fixation. "It is, however, but a step in thought from visual fixation to the fixation of attention" (Boring 1950, 127). His later view was broader, with a more psychological orientation. Braid recognized the great potential of hypnosis.

Braid was one of the first proponents of hypnosis to commend the virtues of self hypnosis. He cited experiments in which patients hypnotized, manipulated, and then awakened themselves. Braid simply asked them to rub their own eyes. They experienced the same results a hypnotist could bring about. This proved, he believed, that hypnosis emanates from the mind of the individual subject, not from the power of the hypnotist. Braid's theory was contrary to the mesmerists' view that the power emanated from the operator. Braid helped evolve hypnosis from its mystical context for use in medicine and psychotherapy.

Fluidists Vs Animists

During these years (1840-1860) many people in England, France, and Germany worked with and theorized about hypnosis. A quarrel developed between two groups: the fluidists inspired by Mesmer, and the animists who followed Braid. The fluidists believed changes in the subject are due to physical effects of fluids emanating from the magnetizers, whereas the animists said everything depended on the changes induced in the subject's mental states. To the animists, physiological changes were obtained through mental factors in the subject. (Janet 1925, 159)

Hypnosis for Anesthesia

Scottish physician James Esdaile (1808-1859) performed thousands of minor operations and 300 major surgical procedures in India using hypnosis as the only anesthesia. Remarkably, patients felt comfortable throughout the procedures and experienced no side effects from the anesthesia. The British government proved to be more open-minded than the medical profession.

A letter to the Medical board describing his work remained unanswered, but a later report to the government, after he had more than 100 cases to describe, led to the appointment of a committee of investigation. The report of the committee was cautious but favorable to further research, and the government accordingly in 1846 established a small Mesmeric hospital in Calcutta where Esdaile might continue his work. (Boring 1950, 123)

Although funding from the Indian government did not last long, official visitors to the hospital were convinced that mesmerism was effective as an anesthetic and partially effective in reducing post-operative shock. Esdaile demonstrated medical applications for mesmerism, which spread to English hospitals.

But the discovery of ether in 1846 and chloroform in 1847 set back the use of hypnosis as anesthesia for many decades. At first people were slow to accept the usefulness of ether and chloroform. P.T. Barnum exploited nitrous oxide's effects for theatrical entertainment in shows. Erickson (1961) pointed out the paradox that during the period when hypnosis was popular, entertainers and charlatans were pushing anesthesia. Once ether and chloroform were accepted, the reverse became true. Chemical anesthesia became the accepted mode in medical use and hypnosis was exploited. For twenty years hypnosis was either conducted by stage hypnotists or else performed secretly. Reputable scientists no longer dared openly study hypnosis. Despite these public setbacks, hypnosis continued to quietly evolve into a legitimate practice for healing and benefiting humanity.

Charcot: Hypnosis as Hysteria

Jean Martin Charcot (1825-1893), founder of the Salpêtrière School, was a physician who treated nervous disorders. He attempted to research hypnosis strictly scientifically. Charcot narrowed his study of hypnosis to observable physiological manifestations, the movements and reflexes of his subjects. He considered the psychological dimension dangerous and unscientific, calling this "minor hypnosis." His view is reminiscent of the behaviorist stand toward psychotherapy where only observable behaviors are considered scientific material. Mental experiences cannot be proven and therefore are out of the scope for behavior therapy.

The dimension that Charcot approved and classified he called "major hypnosis." He developed exact classifications of phenomena according to three reactions: lethargy, catalepsy, and somnambulism. With lethargy the subject's eyes closed as they went into profound unresponsive slumber. In catalepsy eyes opened suddenly and limbs retained any position imposed by the experimenter. During somnambulism subjects could hear, speak, and manifest readiness to accept suggestions.

Charcot's research was based upon work with his patients. The best subjects proved to be female hysterics. This led him to believe that hypnosis was a pathological state. Despite or perhaps because of his cautious conception of hypnosis, Charcot was able to gain acceptance for his hypnotic research in 1881 from the same academy that had rejected Mesmer years before. This decision broke down the condemnation of hypnosis and allowed practitioners to come out of hiding.

Liébeault, Bernheim, and the Nancy School: Hypnosis as Suggestion

Ambroise-Auguste Liébeault (1823-1904) was a humanitarian, providing free medical hypnosis to thousands of patients suffering from many physical symptoms. He was reputed by Bramwell to have successfully hypnotized over 8000 hospital patients. He is considered by some to be the real father of modern hypnosis. Liébeault believed that hypnosis could favorably influence both functional and organic disease. He claimed cures for numerous physical disorders.

Hippolyte Bernheim (1840-1919) heard that Liébeault cured a stubborn case of sciatica which Bernheim had tried unsuccessfully to cure. Curious to confirm this, Bernheim traveled to Liébeault's clinic. He was amazed by Liébeault's abilities and undertook a study of hypnosis with the master which became the major dedication for his life. Bernheim's book, *Hypnosis & Suggestion in Psychotherapy* (1973) that followed from his studies with Liébeault, along with his own research, became the foundation of a major movement in hypnosis, the Nancy School.

Bernheim believed the whole explanation of hypnotic phenomena lies in suggestion. He defined suggestion as influence exerted by a suggested idea and received by the mind. An idea initiated in the mind gives rise to a corresponding sensation in the body. The phenomenon occurs automatically without thinking about it. Everyone experiences this daily, with characteristic facial expressions and body gestures accompanying emotions. For example, when someone mentions a tart lemon we automatically salivate. If we are happy, we smile. Bernheim called these phenomena instinctual acts. "It is impossible to be seized by a vivid idea without the whole body being placed in harmony with this idea" (Bernheim 1973, 129). This central concept in Bernheim's thought marks the origination of the Ideomotor Theory, central to hypnosis and self hypnosis today. (See Chapter 5)

Bernheim believed that during hypnosis, attention is distracted and consciousness is dulled, permitting automatic responses to occur involuntarily. In trance, the subject's transformation of thought into action, sensation, movement, or vision is quickly and actively accomplished. Rational inhibition has no time to interact. Unlike some hypnotists who thought that conscious activity is completely paralyzed, Bernheim saw the ego involved as an observer. For example, a patient in hypnosis could not open his eyes. Upon awakening he said he heard everything but could not prevent his hands from raising and his eyes from closing. Bernheim strongly held that weakening of the will is not the central force in hypnosis: The mechanism of suggestion is the determiner.

There is an increase of this reflex ideomotor, ideosensitive, and ideosensorial excitability. With hypnotism the ideo-reflex excitability is increased in the brain so that any idea received is immediately transformed into an act, without the controlling portion of the brain, the higher centers, being able to prevent the transformation. (Bernheim 1973, 138)

Bernheim compared hypnosis to sleep. He theorized that sleep, whether artificial (hypnosis) or spontaneous, is a cerebral condition that focuses reasoning faculties. The nervous system fixates upon images or suggested ideas. Sleep favors the production of suggestions by suppressing or weakening the moderating influence.

Bernheim had a theory of posthypnotic suggestion as well. Posthypnotic suggestion involves carrying out a suggestion given during trance after awakening. Bernheim believed that hypnotic subjects are conscious of what they are doing while asleep. However, these thoughts are not conscious after awakening. They remain dormant and are recallable when the subject returns to the hypnotic state. When subjects execute a posthypnotic suggestion, they experience themselves having a new idea. Actually, subjects lost the memory of the idea they had in trance. The posthypnotic suggestion is stored in the mind during sleep and remains as a latent potential to act when awake.

Bernheim worked with hundreds of hypnotic patients. The Nancy School inspired many others to work with hypnosis, firmly establishing it as a viable therapeutic method.

Return to Animal Magnetism

Animal magnetism reappeared with Alfred Binet (also author of the early intelligence tests) and Charles Feré's book, *Animal Magnetism* (1888). They performed careful research, empirically testing the effects of magnets on hypnotic subjects. They magnetized patients with a hidden magnet, and trance occurred. They used wooden magnets and nothing happened. They believed that the element of suggestion and expectant attention had been removed by their experiments. These and many other empirical tests convinced them that suggestion had nothing to do with hypnotic effects.

Modern research in expectancy has shown that experimenter bias can alter results even if the experimenter tries to appear neutral. This may have had an influence on their findings. However, in a recent study an experimenter used the passing of hands method of magnetism and found that deeper trances occurred with this method than when traditional techniques were employed. (Pulos 1980) Today a form of therapy called Transcranial Magnetic Stimulation (TMS) passes a magnetic field across the brain. This treatment is used therapeutically with depression and bipolar disorder. Magnets are also used to help people with pain. These uses of magnetism open possibilities for further research.

Auto-Suggestion and the Neo-Nancy School

By the early 1900's, self hypnosis had not been explored very much, with the exception of Braid's work in the 1800's. In Braid's view, hypnotic phenomena occur in the mind of the subject, not from the hypnotist. These concepts, though not inconsistent with Bernheim's theory, remained undeveloped by the Nancy School.

Emil Coué (1857-1926), influenced by Liébeault, founded the Neo-Nancy School in 1910. He used self suggestion. As a pharmacist for twenty-five years, Coué gave suggestions to accompany his customers' drug orders. He observed and thought about the implications of the positive results from his use of suggestion. He believed that all suggestions ultimately became auto-suggestions patients give to themselves. Finally at age fifty-five, Coué introduced an approach that abandoned trance entirely and worked with waking auto-suggestion. He hoped to free people from dependence on another person as their hypnotist, to foster independence and self mastery.

Coué's method was based on consciously harnessing the effects of auto-suggestion he believed stemmed from the imagination. He distinguished between will power and imagination. Our actions do not spring from our will, as we might expect, but from our imagination. Any effort to bring about a change must begin in the imagination.

Coué developed an uncomplicated system that taught people how to harness their imagination through self-suggestion. He gave patients some simple ideas to vividly imagine each morning, such as: "Day by day, in every way, I am getting better and better." (Coué 1923, 101) He encouraged people to imagine the positive results they wanted to achieve and stop trying to will themselves to accomplish them.

Coué believed that we have two selves: the conscious and the unconscious. The conscious possesses an unreliable memory while the unconscious recalls perfectly, in minute detail. The unconscious regulates our organs and acts as mediator of all our functions whatever they are. This is synonymous with imagination, which always makes us act.

The key to directing the unconscious yourself is through the use of auto-suggestion. Bernheim had defined suggestion as the act of imposing an idea on the brain of another. But Coué believed that suggestions are only effective if the subject transforms them into auto-suggestions. Many modern self hypnosis practitioners apply variations of these same principles today.

Baudouin: Auto-Suggestion with Trance

Charles Baudouin developed a theory of auto-suggestion and self hypnosis drawn from Coué's theory of auto-suggestion, but unlike Coué, he included trance. His classic book, *Suggestion and Auto-Suggestion* (1921) is one of the few that develops an in-depth theory of self suggestion. Baudouin defined suggestion as the subconscious realization of an idea. This takes place in three phases: modification, unconscious realization, and the appearance of the modification that has been thought.

People give themselves auto-suggestions constantly throughout the day without realizing it. These auto-suggestions act to influence what a person can or cannot accomplish. This influence works according to three laws. First, the **Law of Concentrated Attention** states that if spontaneous attention is concentrated on an idea, it tends to realize itself. Spontaneous attention is like that of a child, or when a bright color catches the eye. This is distinguished from voluntary and reflective attention where we focus on something by choice.

The second law, the **Law of Auxiliary Emotion** holds that when an idea is enveloped in a powerful emotion, there is more likelihood that this idea will be suggestively realized. This occurs because spontaneous attention dwells on anything that is emotionally compelling. For example, our son greatly enjoyed a hobby with radio controlled cars as a child. Now he has found himself interested in engineering, with a special interest in model construction.

The third law, the **Law of Reversed Effort** was one of Coué's most important contributions according to Baudouin.

When an idea imposes itself on the mind to such an extent as to give rise to a suggestion, all the conscious efforts which the subject makes in order to counteract this suggestion are not merely without the desired effect, but they actually run counter to the subject's conscious wishes and tend to intensify the suggestion. (Baudouin 1921, 137)

Because of the Law of Reversed Effort, it is impossible to give an auto-suggestion without creating a negative counter-suggestion. This law explains why people have difficulty carrying out new year's resolutions, staying on diets, or following an exercise program.

Whenever we concentrate voluntary attention on an idea, which implies making an effort, I am simultaneously conscious of an action toward this idea, and of a resistance in consequence of which the idea continually escapes me...Thus when we concentrate on an idea, we do not think a single idea but two conflicting ideas which

*result in two conflicting suggestions which neutralize each
other. (Baudouin 1921, 146)*

A paradox emerges: how to make a deliberate effort to
change? Baudouin found the solution in self hypnosis. During
hypnosis people are relaxed and yet focused. Under these
circumstances, ideas can be accepted as suggestions without the
reverse resistance occurring. Baudouin gave detailed instructions
for entering self hypnosis, followed by self administered auto-
suggestions. When consciousness is riveted on a single idea in
trance, reverse suggestions cannot dominate the person.

Psychoanalysis and Hypnosis

Josef Breuer introduced psychoanalytic applications of
hypnotic therapy. Previous emphasis of hypnosis had been direct
symptom removal. With his patient, Anna O., Breuer discovered
the original trauma related to her hysterical symptoms could be
brought to the surface of consciousness by hypnosis, resulting in
cure. Janet simultaneously arrived at the technique of liberating
repressed emotions associated with traumatic memories, but
Breuer is given historic credit for the discovery.

Sigmund Freud (1856-1939) became fascinated with
hypnosis and studied it ardently. He translated both Charcot and
Bernheim's books into German. His interest was so intense that
he traveled to Nancy to visit Bernheim and Liébeault and brought
one of his patients with him for Bernheim to hypnotize. He
published a book with Breuer entitled *Studien Uber Hysterie* in
1895. They stated:

The individual hysterical symptoms immediately disappeared without returning if we succeed in thoroughly awakening the memories of the causal process with its accompanying affects, and if the patient circumstantially discussed the process in the most detailed manner and gave verbal expression to the affect. (Wolberg 1948, 11)

They concluded that symptoms developed as a result of experiences so damaging to the individual that the memory was repressed. Energy became blocked in unconscious conflict. Freud used hypnosis and suggestion as a method to release blocked energy and thereby cure patients.

At first Freud used suggestion and hypnosis as his primary technique until one patient, Lucy R., was unable to go into trance. Freud remembered that Bernheim's patients often recalled their trance experiences when awake. Freud recognized the potential. He decided to try encouraging Lucy to say every thought that came to mind, hoping she would express her unconscious conflict. His difficulty with inducing trance led him to develop an alternative technique, free association, to accomplish the therapeutic catharsis that hypnosis had brought about.

He eventually expanded his view of symptoms: They were not only manifestations of repressed instinctive strivings, they were also defenses against these strivings. Including counterforces led him to reject the use of hypnosis for removal of symptoms, since he believed that symptoms served a purpose. Freud's rejection of hypnosis had little to do with questioning the potency or validity of hypnosis as a psychological tool. Rather, Freud had great difficulty incorporating hypnosis into his psychoanalytic therapy. Freud's rejection was based upon:

His difficulty inducing the hypnotic state in a high percentage of patients, inability to produce and maintain posthypnotic reactions of a therapeutic nature, and the intensification of both transference and countertransference reactions elicited through the hypnotic relationship (Kline 1958, viii).

Freud's hypnotic technique, unfortunately, was primitive, using only suggestion through direct methods. Although Freud dismissed hypnosis from psychoanalysis, he drew many of his concepts from hypnosis. Later, psychoanalysts reincorporated hypnosis to facilitate the analytic process.

Dissociation Theorists: Janet, Sidis, & James

Pierre Janet (1859-1947), a student of Charcot's, believed that the abandonment of hypnosis arose out of the controversy between the Salpêtrière School and the Nancy School. Charcot had given hypnosis medical acceptance by delimiting it to a physiological affect, thus placing it within the province of the medical profession. Bernheim viewed it as a mental phenomenon which meant it fell under the psychological realm. Although the Nancy School was victorious, their triumph was at great cost to hypnosis. Psychology as yet had no credibility to the medical establishment. Research and practice of hypnosis declined for many years. Nonetheless, Janet continued to uphold hypnosis as an effective mode of treatment for neurosis. He stated,

If my work is not accepted today, it will be tomorrow, when there will be a new turn to fashion's wheel, which is

going to bring back hypnotism as surely as our grandmother's styles. (Janet 1925, 151)

Janet was a central figure in the history of hypnosis, influencing many with his books. He theorized that complexes of ideas exist split off or dissociated from personality. Through hypnosis these dissociated thoughts and experiences could become part of consciousness once again.

Janet believed that hypnosis was not a state of sleep, nor should it be characterized as suggestibility. Hypnosis belonged to the group of somnambulisms, a modification of the normal mental state. The modification was considered a temporary state in which the individual's personal memory is dissociated. Hypnosis not only arrests the normal personality, but also develops other tendencies that vary from person to person. (Janet, 1924)

He believed one way we can discern the difference between a state of hypnosis and a normal state is that hypnosis involves a modification of personal memory, while in everyday life personal memory is continuous. He cited an example: Though he might be tired and depressed, he still remembered how he felt earlier when he was not feeling tired and depressed. But in trance these conscious balances and tendencies are replaced by repressed tendencies. Another life, another character, another memory can be evoked in place of the usual one. For this reason, hypnosis can be useful in working with neurosis, since it gives patients an opportunity to experience something apart from their everyday tensions and problems. Secondly, hypnosis can activate dissociated parts of the personality Janet called "tendencies." Ordinarily, unused tendencies atrophy. During trance these tendencies can be reintegrated into the waking personality (Janet 1924, 147).

Janet believed patients often exhibit imbalances in their energy levels. Some patients need to be stimulated to balance their deficits. Other patients require calming to help them be less excitable, more balanced. Hypnosis could be used to bring this about. Individual tendencies should be taken into account.

Janet's hypnotic theory anticipated many of the ideas in modern hypnosis when he stated that the unconscious mind is a reservoir of untapped potential beyond the limits of conscious awareness. His clinical observations are a useful source of insight.

Boris Sidis (1898), a Harvard University researcher, attempted to unify the views from the Salpêtrière and Nancy Schools:

With the Nancy School, we agree that suggestion is all-powerful in hypnotic trance; the hypnotic trance is in fact, a state of heightened suggestibility, or, rather of pure reflex consciousness; but with the Paris School, we agree that a changed physiological state is a prerequisite to hypnosis, and this modification consists in the disaggregation of the superior from the inferior centres, in the segregation of the controlling consciousness from the reflex consciousness. (Sidis 1898, 70)

Sidis carried Janet's perspective further, of hypnosis as dissociation. The higher conscious levels of controls were dissociated from the reflexes and automatic lower levels. During hypnosis the normal course of an idea is inhibited; a suggested movement or idea is carried through without interruption from the conscious mind.

William James (1842-1910) was also influenced by Janet's hypnotic theory. In the normal waking state, James believed people have their consciousness and their subliminal consciousness. "In hypnosis, waking consciousness is split off from the rest of the nervous system while subliminal consciousness is laid bare and comes into direct contact with the external world." (James, in Taylor 1982, 42) This secondary consciousness is intelligent as well, attending to its own concerns without interfering with active consciousness. Everyday awareness could be but an extract of a vast and greater reality, "beyond the margin" (Taylor 1982, 42). James pointed to a realm of potential outside consciousness.

Unlike Janet, James believed suggestibility was the main indicator of hypnosis. In trance the subject develops motor capability, so that ideas can easily be translated to ideomotor and ideosensory excitability, leading to action. Suggestibility also causes the field of consciousness to narrow by introducing one idea that produces an intense emotional response. All other ideas are banished, creating a state of focused concentration.

Munro & Bramwell:
Hypnosis as a Positive Mental Tool

The early 1900's marked a period when the medical model predominated. Psychotherapy was struggling to become an accepted treatment. Some doctors saw the importance of the mind and attempted to persuade other medical professionals to include mental processes in their work. Henry S. Munro was an example. He was a medical doctor who lectured around the country to other doctors about the value of what he termed "Suggestive Therapeutics." He tried to show that psychotherapy could be an important adjunct to clinical work that doctors should recognize and use to improve their effectiveness. For Munro, psychotherapy was synonymous with hypnosis and suggestion, occurring through three basic methods: hypnotic suggestion, waking suggestion, and persuasion, reasoning, or re-education. He emphasized that it is of vital importance for all good psychological treatment to be accompanied by teaching patients healthy habits to unify mind and body. He was a forerunner in proposing the concept of preventive medicine. He also emphasized the value of being an ethical physician committed to the welfare of his patients.

Suggestion was central to Munro's view. In order for a suggestion to be assimilated as a self-suggestion, people need a mental attitude of conviction.

This mental attitude evokes or calls forth latent powers or inherent psychic activities, and renders the reserve energy available or useless as he has confidence or lack of confidence. (Munro 1911, 145)

Energy reserves could influence physiological processes and help in healing the body. Suggestion along with a positive mental attitude could promote healing and health, similar to positive thinking approaches popular today. Munro encouraged the family and friends of his patients to create a positive, suggestive environment.

Bramwell helped revive the concept of self hypnosis. He pointed out that "The essential characteristic of the hypnotic state is the subject's far-reaching power over his own organism. (Bramwell 1903, 437) He encouraged applications to medicine and described suggestion theory, sympathizing with Braid. In his comprehensive assessment he was hopeful that hypnosis could help in curing and preventing disease, alleviating pain, and assisting medical treatment (Bramwell 1903, 439). His hopes were well founded.

⌘

Despite the efforts of these fine hypnotic researchers, many doctors of the early period continued to consider hypnosis unscientific. Again, unfortunately, the benefits of hypnosis were disregarded, until World War I, when many soldiers suffered from injuries and the trauma of war. Hypnotherapy was revived to facilitate therapy of shell shock and other conditions. Numerous accounts of rapid and effective treatment were given during this period, which led to renewed interest in hypnosis, laying a foundation for a new era of hypnosis.

Two

Modern History

Because the historical past, unlike the natural past, is a living past, kept alive by the act of historical thinking itself, the historical change from one way of thinking to another is not the death of the first, but its survival integrated in a new context involving the development and criticism of its own ideas.

--Collingwood, 1957

A s hypnosis entered the modern era it was used as an adjunct to psychotherapy. Modern researchers also took an interest in hypnosis, conducting experiments to help expand understanding of the phenomena.

Hypnoanalysis

Psychoanalysts began to use hypnosis for therapy as hypnoanalysis. Patients were put into trance and regressed to a time period when a damaging or traumatic experience occurred. They could relive the event and liberate associated emotions, shortening the lengthy period analysis can require.

One of the most famous accounts of hypnoanalysis was Lindner's hypnoanalysis of a criminal psychopath. He tape recorded all the sessions and carefully recounted the treatment process. The patient relived traumas he endured as an infant.

Lindner described the process as:

Equivalent to a surgical removal of barriers and hazards, that it pierces the psychic substrata and raises the repressed to the level of awareness (Wolberg 1948, 16).

Renowned professor, writer, and practitioner Lewis R. Wolberg divided hypnotic phenomena into induction phase, trance phase, and post hypnotic period. Trance cannot be explained by psychological or physiological theory alone. Instead, hypnosis involves a complex psychosomatic reaction including both psychological and physiological aspects. The physiological aspect involves inhibiting rational faculties. These higher brain functions are suspended by hypnosis, allowing the ego to link with subcortical systems. As a result, hypnotic subjects can control various organs and somatic functions they cannot usually control in the waking state.

The psychological aspect of hypnosis is an analytical process whereby the patient is led on a journey of self discovery. Using special trance skills such as regression and exploration of unconscious experiences, patients can bring up deep insight about their difficulties and work them through for healthier functioning.

Modern Quests: Hypnosis Research

Pavlov

Ivan Pavlov (1849-1936), the Russian researcher who was famous for his formulations of stimulus-response conditioning, also did extensive studies of hypnosis and suggestion. He formulated a physiological theory. Pavlov believed that the cerebral cortex influences the entire organism in a complex manner he called the primary signaling system. All animals have this signaling system to maintain balance between organism and environment. Human beings distinguish themselves from animals through what Pavlov called the secondary signaling system of higher thinking and speech. Language is a conditioned stimulus affecting the processes of the higher nervous activity. One person's words can powerfully affect another:

A word is as real a conditioned stimulus for man as all the other stimuli in common with animals, but at the same time more all-inclusive than any other stimuli (Platonov 1959, 15).

Language influences action only after there has been pairing of words with unconditioned responses. Words become signals. For example, the word "hurt" acquires definite meaning for a child only when it is combined with real pain at least once. Then the verbal stimulus of the word can evoke a pain response due to the bond formed.

Pavlov defined hypnosis as a reflex of the brain. Based upon numerous experiments with animals, Pavlov concluded that sleep is brought on by higher division of the central nervous system. After exhaustion of the cortex from the waking state, inhibition replaces excitation, giving the cells a chance to be restored. During hypnosis, as in natural sleep, internal inhibition spreads over the cerebral cortex. Lighter trances, as in partial sleep, occur when some parts of the cerebral cortex undergo inhibitory response while others do not. Scattered areas of sleep take place in a complex pattern throughout the cortex. Pavlov thought this accounts for the individualized different levels of hypnosis that occur.

Suggestion and auto-suggestion are based upon the transition of certain cortical cells to an inhibitory state while others are selectively stimulated. A suggestion or auto-suggestion stimulates a reflex in the brain, bringing about an intensified response. Pavlov's theory led to useful links between hypnosis and learning theory, but was only part of the puzzle.

Hull

Clark Hull (1884-1952) attempted to give a scientific account of hypnosis through the modern experimental method. Only careful research could give hypnosis acceptance from the scientific community as well as answer some of the many questions about the nature of hypnosis.

Hull set up a laboratory at Yale University where he tested many aspects of hypnosis. He performed hundreds of experiments on hypnotic suggestion and waking suggestion. Hull tested and compared some of the conflicting theories to explain the phenomena: hypnosis as dissociation, hypnosis as sleep, and hypnosis as habit.

Hull's work led him to draw certain conclusions about the fundamentals of hypnosis. He discovered rapport to be an inherent and essential characteristic of hypnosis. He also believed hypersuggestibility distinguished hypnosis. The change in suggestibility was a measurable verification of hypnosis. Hull thought his research disproved three classical theories: hypnosis as a form of sleep, as a pathological condition related to hysteria, and as a state of dissociation. However, his conclusions were not universally accepted. Hull abandoned hypnotic research and returned to the psychology of learning theory.

Hilgard

Ernest Hilgard, eminent professor and prominent researcher in the field of psychology, was extensively involved in hypnotic research since 1957. He states that his interest in hypnosis was:

To see hypnosis "domesticated" as a part of normal psychology, on the assumption that understanding of the normal human mind and behavior will be enhanced if hypnosis is taken seriously along with perception, learning, motivation, and the other accepted topics of general psychology (Hilgard, 1977).

Hilgard's research integrated hypnotic understandings with motivation, learning, memory, and perception. He is well known for development of the Stanford Hypnotic Susceptibility Scales. The relative hypnotizability of individuals can be determined based upon their suggestibility tests scores. Hilgard believed a certain percentage of people have genetic talents with hypnosis, just as some people are athletically, musically, or artistically gifted. Hilgard believed this talent was relatively constant. He differed from Erickson who believed that all people can be developed in hypnotic skills despite different hypnotizability ratings.

Hilgard explored Janet's ideas on dissociation and developed a neodissociation theory. He evolved Janet's theory further by recognizing that dissociation need not be neurotic. Hilgard believed all people, healthy and neurotic alike, always experience more than one thing at a time. In hypnosis this is exaggerated and can thereby deepen our understanding of the workings of attention, memory, perception, creativity, imagination, etc. Hilgard theorized people have what he called a "hidden observer." Even though a person thinks he does not recall anything about an experience in trance, there is a part, a hidden observer, who does indeed recall everything. Dissociation is also central in pain control, an area he carefully researched and developed applications for people to use.

Hilgard believed, in agreement with Erickson, that hypnosis is a true state in and of itself. His many research subjects were able to differentiate a distinct experience of trance, which convinced him that trance is more than hypersuggestibility, though heightened suggestibility is part of it. Through many years of rigorous experimental research Hilgard influenced the course of hypnosis in a positive way. He led it away from the weird, the mystical, and the neurotic, into the realm of the psychological.

Orne

Martin Orne, another important hypnosis researcher also theorized that hypnosis is a state and attempted to empirically demonstrate and define its parameters.

Orne differentiated the genuinely hypnotized subject, *reals*, from the hypnotic simulator by their use of a way of thinking and perceiving he called *trance logic*. Erickson also confirmed that the logic of the hypnotized person is different from a person who is awake. Orne theorized hypnotic subjects are influenced by environmental expectations, *demand characteristics*, of the situation. His work explored both the psychological and socio-logical bases for hypnosis. The Johns Hopkins research on

32

psychotherapy at Phipps Clinic utilized this as one of the bases for comparison of similar effectiveness ratings among apparently widely differing approaches to psychotherapy (Frank, Hoehn-Saric, Imber, Liberman, Stone, 1978).

Orne's research showed that reals demonstrated higher tolerance to pain than simulators, performed posthypnotic acts more readily, and were dehypnotized more slowly. Orne concluded that hypnosis is a genuine phenomenon with distinct characterisics. Certain qualities of trance cannot be faked.

Sarbin & Coe

Several researchers, Theodore Sarbin and William Coe, offered a different model of hypnosis as a form of role-taking. Subjects learn to act as the role of a hypnotized person. Sarbin believed that a theory of hypnosis must account for four major phenomena: dissociation of behavior, automatic response, how such a magnitude of response can follow from mere spoken instructions, and individual differences in response to hypnosis. They believed that role-taking theory, enacted at a very high level of organismic involvement, explains these hypnotic phenomena as a social drama. Successful role-taking depends upon favorable motivation, role perception, and role-taking aptitude. A successful hypnotic subject is highly motivated, has a clear perception of how he or she should act as a hypnotic subject, and wants to be deeply involved in this role. This view of hypnosis deletes the magical element and makes it explainable, measurable, and understandable in a sociological context. But some phenomena cannot be accounted for by this theory.

Barber

Theodore Barber, another contemporary theorist and researcher contended that hypnosis is not a state or trance at all, nor is hypnosis hypersuggestibility. Barber considers hypnosis a special interaction between hypnotist and subject. He views the subject as hopeful and highly expectant about the situation, thus open to being led in a structured experience. Barber calls this *perceptual-cognitive restructuring.*

All of these theories, although helpful and important in understanding and researching hypnotic phenomena, offer partial explanations of hypnosis. We agree with Josephine Hilgard, co-researcher and wife of Ernest Hilgard, when she points to the inevitable limitations of "nothing-but" theories of hypnosis. Hypnosis is a complex phenomenon and must be explained by multivaried factors on psychological, physiological, and sociological levels. All the views of hypnosis can contribute to our understanding and application of hypnosis, (Hilgard 1970, 249) but one must be wary not to oversimplify just to be parsimonious: Occam's razor can shave too close.

Hypnosis As a Therapeutic Tool

Shaffer

G. Wilson Shaffer wrote and worked extensively with hypnosis over many years. His ideas from the 1940's and 50's are now being rediscovered. Shaffer pointed out that the person's *mental set* is important in inducing and using hypnosis. To a certain extent, our past thinking determines whether suggestions will be accepted and how they will be responded to.

Subjects always have a choice in their response: it is not

under the control of the hypnotist. Hypnosis occurs in a relationship. Shaffer believed that hypnosis is always voluntary. Hypnotized subjects cannot be forced to do something that conflicts with their values and beliefs.

Shaffer believed that the authenticity of hypnosis need not be questioned. He wanted hypnosis to be demystified and used for psychotherapy. He developed ways of giving patients support and positive learning experiences with hypnosis.

Weitzenhoffer

Andre Weitzenhoffer postulated that the differences between hypnotic and waking phenomena are essentially qualitative, not quantitative. Suggestibility was the key factor. He wrote several comprehensive books and clinical teaching manuals on hypnosis, carefully detailing mechanisms of suggestion with applications.

Unlike Shaffer, Weitzenhoffer believed the subject is the reactive, passive participant in the hypnotic process. He called hypnotic behavior *non voluntary* or *involuntary*. He believed hypnosis was:

A condition or state of selective hypersuggestibility brought about in an individual subject through the use of certain specific psychological or physical manipulations of the individual by another person (hypnotist) (Weitzenhoffer 1957, 32).

Weitzenhoffer extended his definition to self hypnosis since the self can take the role of both hypnotist and subject.

Indirect Hypnotherapy

Milton Erickson was the founder of the Indirect Method of hypnosis, a sophisticated modern approach with timeless roots. Indirect hypnosis draws upon much of the history discussed above, but also has unique contributions of its own. Erickson developed his model of hypnosis from a lifetime of experiments he performed to investigate the nature of hypnosis. His formal research began during a 1923-24 seminar on hypnosis under Clark Hull. His first experiment indicated to him Hull's strong conviction that the hypnotist controls the subject's experience was incorrect. Subjects developed deep spontaneous somnambulistic trances quite naturally during periods of introspection. He found that suggestions, rather than serving as commands to be followed, constituted "No more than a point of departure for responsive behavior" (Erickson 1964, 158).

Erickson experimented on thousands of subjects during his years as a therapist. Generally he found that the more simple, permissive, and unobtrusive the technique, the more effective it proved to be both experimentally and therapeutically. Erickson observed that:

The less the operator does and the more he confidently and expectantly allows the subject to do, the easier and more effectively will the hypnotic state and hypnotic phenomena be elicited in accord with the subject's own capacities and uncolored by efforts to please the operator (Erickson 1964, 161)

Erickson's main conclusion from his research was that hypnotists are unimportant in determining hypnotic results, regardless of their understandings and intentions. "It is what the subject does, not the operator's wishes that determine what shall be the hypnotic manifestation" (Erickson 1964, 162).

Erickson recommended hypnotic research of the future be based on subject evaluations and subject performance rather than on the experimenter's assessment. Erickson's theory implies the possibility for creative learning in self hypnosis.

Numerous volumes continue to be written about Erickson's approach to hypnotherapy. Some of the most relevant major interpretations will be reviewed.

Erickson and Rossi

Ernest Rossi co-authored several books with Erickson. The following passage draws together the basic ideas in Rossi's work with Erickson. Much of the self hypnotic approach we have developed in this book derives from years of study with Erickson and Rossi. We continue to learn and develop our approach from their inspiration. Therefore, we will describe the Erickson-Rossi model in detail.

We view hypnotherapy as a process whereby we help people utilize their own mental associations, memories, and life potentials to achieve their own therapeutic goals. Hypnotic suggestion can facilitate the utilization of abilities and potentials that already exist within a person but that remain unused or underdeveloped because of lack of training or understanding. The hypnotherapist carefully explores a patient's individuality to ascertain what life learnings, experiences, and mental skills are available to deal with the problem. The therapist then facilitates an approach to trance experience wherein the patient may utilize these uniquely personal internal responses to achieve therapeutic goals. (Erickson, Rossi 1979, 1)

The goals of therapy are accomplished through three stages: preparation, therapeutic trance, and ratification. Rossi states this three-stage paradigm is basic to understanding Erickson's clinical work.

Stage I: Preparation

During the first stage, the therapist explores patients' life experiences and encourages a constructive orientation toward therapeutic change. Good rapport is established. Rapport derives from mutual acceptance Rossi (1977) described as *Yes Set*. The therapist interviews the patient to ascertain what early learnings and life experiences are available to use in therapy. These may be hobbies, interests, life roles, mental sets, personality characteristics, mechanisms of defense, or perhaps just the presenting problem of behavior. Similar to Jerome D. Frank's theory (1978), patients have problems because their belief systems and frames of reference are limited. Hypnotherapeutic preparation introduces new potential for attitudes, belief systems, and expectancies. The stage is set for therapy to take place.

Phase II: Therapeutic Trance

The second phase, therapeutic trance, involves trance. People activate their own mental skills and associations to develop trance abilities. Life skills and learnings are used to bring about the hypnotic experience. The content of therapeutic trance varies with each person. Therapeutic trance begins with fixation of attention. Then, the subject's habitual frameworks and belief systems are suspended, to allow for unconscious search processes to happen.

Fixation of attention is widely used for induction, both in history and in current literature. This method is timeless. But Erickson emphasized that fixation does not need to be on a standardized external object. Attention ideally should be fixated on an object of the individual's own inner experience. Since trance is an inwardly directed experience, trance is begun best by redirecting attention to inner, subjective experiencing. Though we all share a common nature, each person is unique. Standardized methods of fixation do not incorporate this individuality: What interests and fascinates one person may not interest another. Erickson (1967) believed that too much attention to externals militates against trance induction, while conversely, use of internal, spontaneous imagery leads more directly to hypnosis. When we focus attention on our own experience and behavior, we find our attention easily becomes fixated. You will notice that many of the exercises in this book encourage following your own inner experiencing, associations, and thoughts. The path to self hypnosis begins within.

After the subject's attention is fixated, the usual mental sets and frames of reference may be *depotentiated*. (Erickson, Rossi, 1979) This means that typical conscious patterns of associations can be temporarily suspended, or "put in brackets" (Husserl, 1964) for a time. Depotentiating mental sets clears a space, allowing new, latent patterns of thoughts, feelings, and attitudes to emerge and become actual.

Creative learning takes place through the mental "gaps" that occur when our typical patterns of association are broken up:

> *A creative moment occurs when a habitual pattern of association is interrupted...the creative moment is thus a gap in one's habitual pattern of awareness. Bartlett (1958) has described how the genesis of original thinking can be understood as the filling in of mental gaps. The new that appears in creative moments is thus the basic unit of original thought and insight as well as personality change (Rossi 1972, 6).*

Erickson and Rossi believed suspension of problematic and limited beliefs permits emergence of new, healthier patterns of response. This position is compatible to that of Lawrence Kubie, renowned psychoanalyst and theorist of creativity who collaborated on some research with Erickson. Kubie stated:

> *The measure of health is flexibility, the freedom to learn through experience, the freedom to change with changing internal and external circumstances...The essence of normality is flexibility in all of these vital ways. The essence of illness is the freezing of behavior into unalterable and insatiable patterns (Kubie 1975, 21).*

To attain an open, receptive mental state, limited perspectives must be set aside. Erickson recognized early in his research that people often have difficulties permitting mental gaps. However, when we become confused, have doubt, face overloads, or get into binds, a gap happens naturally. We tend to resist allowing gaps, but when they happen sometimes, we accept them. Based on these observations, Erickson developed techniques to help clients automatically and naturally let go of their rigid sets in response. He called these techniques indirect suggestions. Indirect techniques of suggestion help people bypass their learned limitations. They also facilitate mental associations and unconscious processes.

The indirect hypnotherapist calls upon a variety of techniques to activate a search within the patient's own repertoire of learnings to make new responses available. The search appeals to many natural mechanisms of mind such as curiosity, filling in meaning for pauses, response to implication, and personalizing a general statement. Metaphors, analogies, puns, and allusions can also stimulate new ideas and a changed perspective, especially in trance.

The hypnotic response is the culmination of the cooperative efforts of hypnotist and patient. It is experienced typically as a surprise, happening by itself. Indeed, the more unconsciously initiated, the more surprising it is. Hypnosis makes a wealth of unusual experiences possible, such as body sensations (heaviness, lightness, hand levitation), immobility, hallucinations, to name just a few. These experiences can initiate new abilities. The response comes from the subject's own background, life experiences, and genetic endowment, yet it represents a different organization and integration: a new response. Because the response is effortless, the learning can be far more powerful.

Troublesome and negative personality traits which tend to remain constant can be utilized for therapeutic purposes. Even a negative quality can be transformed into a positive asset so that the client's self-concept changes to include a more positive way of thinking about him or herself. New creative interpretations and frames of reference permit inner potential to emerge, often surprising the client with better possibilities.

Through the artistry of hypnotherapy, creative personality reconstructions become possible. In chemistry there is a difference between the concept of a mixture and the concept of a compound. Personality traits are similar. Like elements of the chemical molecule of the personality, these traits of personality can combine to form a pattern, a compound of traits. Rather than just resorting themselves into different mixtures, personality traits can integrate as a molecule, with new properties and greater potential.

Erickson and Rossi based this theory on a fundamental principle expressed by Erickson in 1967:

The reality of the deep trance must necessarily be in accord with the fundamental needs and structure of the total personality. Thus, it is that the profoundly neurotic person in the deep trance can, in that situation, be freed from his otherwise overwhelming neurotic behavior, and thereby a foundation laid for his therapeutic reeducation in accord with the fundamental personality. The overlay of neuroticism, however extensive, does not destroy the central core of the personality, though it may disguise and cripple the manifestations of it (Haley 1967, 13).

The unconscious, the central core of the person, is basically healthy. Therefore, neurotic problems do not need to be consciously analyzed. The therapeutic process frees and strengthens the naturally healthy part of the personality to experience, respond, act, and learn.

In an earlier book, Rossi (1972) conceptualized the unconscious as the source of creativity. He stated that negative, troubling symptoms are actually the beginnings of positive change yet to come. Erickson believed trance reeducation returns patients to their own natural unconscious functioning which restores them to the wellsprings of their personality.

Therapeutic trance can initiate small changes. The small changes can be subtle, like lessening the intensity, duration, or frequency of a symptom. These beginnings gain momentum and start other changes that ripple through the system. Incorporating the patient's world of meanings helps to make the small changes relevant and helpful in altering the patient's difficulty.

Phase Three: Ratification

Trance ratification can be a powerful indicator that something important has taken place. Ideomotor phenomena can act as a trance ratifier for the patient to experience. This helps confirm trance learnings and acts as an integrative process. Many people do not recognize when they are in a trance since the unconscious is activated and the conscious is dissociated.

Ideomotor and ideosensory phenomena link thought and action, symbolizing the natural ease with which people find themselves automatically behaving differently. This confirms that they have indeed experienced something different.

Erickson and Rossi developed many subtle intricacies of indirect suggestion and its applications for numerous psychological disorders. Trance has rich potential to give new experiences and throw doubt on past assumptions of limitations.

This guides people to reinterpret themselves more positively so that problems either dissolve or can be resolved with new strengths, strategies, and renewed hope.

Haley

Jay Haley developed many of his concepts of strategic family therapy from studies he did with Erickson. Haley explained Erickson through a communication theory which he developed earlier with Gregory Bateson. His interpretation of Erickson's work emphasizes certain qualities and de-emphasize others.

In 1952 Haley and his associates applied the Russell-Whitehead theory of logical types to psychotherapy (Sluzki and Ransom, 1976). The thesis of Haley's theory is that there is a discontinuity between a class and its members. The class cannot be a member of itself nor can a member be the class. The class is at a different level of abstraction, a different logical type. This led to the discovery that learning is not a single level phenomenon. A person also learns how to learn. Paradox can arise out of this. The classic example is from Epimenides: "I am lying." Is he telling the truth?

This paradox can occur because a negative statement classifying another negative statement occurs in a single message so that the class and its member are self-referent and the discontinuity between the two classes is breached (Sluzki and Ransom 1976, 60).

Bateson applied the theory of logical types to communication. He saw humans as classifying beings who label their communicative messages, generating paradoxes at times. A message that qualifies another message at another level of abstraction is defined as a *meta-message*. Metacommunications are at a higher level of abstraction and are thus communicated implicitly.

Another concept they developed was framing. Framing is exemplified by the logical paradox:

[All statements written within this frame are untrue]

In communications, one person indicates with a framing message how subsequent messages are to be received.

The fuller description included the idea that when one person communicates two levels of message to another when these levels both qualify and conflict with each other, the other person is faced with an impossible situation. He cannot respond to either level without violating a prohibition at the other level, so he is wrong whatever he does. The bind becomes complete when the "victim" cannot leave the field or comment upon his impossible situation (Sluzki and Ransom 1976, 68).

Haley (1963, 1967, 1972) described Erickson as a master of strategy, comparing Erickson's hypnotherapy to the process of logical paradox itself. In trance induction the subject is directed to go into trance and voluntarily produce phenomena that are supposed to be involuntary, e.g. in a hand levitation the subject's hand raises seemingly by itself. The subject does not feel in control of this movement. According to Haley, there is a paradox here. The hypnotist is imposing incongruent directives: The subject has voluntarily come for hypnosis, and thus does not want to leave the session. Yet, the options are contradictory; to follow the hypnotist's directive to deliberately act spontaneously. This is a classic double bind situation.

Haley compared paradox to most forms of psychotherapy. In psychoanalysis the patient is directed to spontaneously free associate. Generally, the patient does certain things he is directed to do as part of therapy, yet the changes that occur do not follow directly from the voluntary acts but somehow spontaneously take place when the time is right.

Haley developed his own approach from his interpretation of Erickson's methods for dealing with resistance. The therapist's job, according to Haley, is to maneuver the patient from symptomatic patterns to healthy ones. Erickson utilized resistance as part of therapy. If the patient had a symptom, Erickson would focus on how the patient used the symptom, to find better ways. Haley saw this as a maneuver to get control:

The subject is thereby caught in a situation where his resistance is defined as cooperative behavior. He finds himself following the hypnotist's directives no matter what he does, because what he does is defined as cooperative. (Haley 1973, 24)

This is one type of utilization. Whatever the client presented, Erickson accepted and used, altering it ever so slightly to bring about the beginnings of change. Erickson used the analogy of the course of a river:

If he opposes the river by trying to block it, the river will merely go over and around him. But if he accepts the river and diverts it in a new direction, the force of the river will cut a new channel (Haley 1973, 25).

These concepts of strategic interventions from a hypnotist can be relevant to self hypnosis. Applications can be made in terms of the attitude you take toward yourself in working with self hypnosis. The Ericksonian approach encourages you not to fight against your nature. Learn to use what you have. Undiscovered talents and resources are already there within you. Exercises throughout the book offer opportunities to become aware of your individual response and follow it. In this way, change evolves naturally and effectively.

Self Hypnosis Today

The evolution of hypnosis has been sketched from its early historical roots, when practitioners had to fight for the right to even practice hypnosis, to modern hypnosis which has developed into an accepted discipline. Self hypnosis has also grown in acceptance and has many practitioners today. Each modern theory draws from one or more of the early theories of hypnosis described in the history. Creative techniques follow naturally from theory. All draw from the wellspring of classic hypnosis.

⌘

Many varied aspects of hypnosis are included in this book, presenting a broad spectrum of techniques. You can experiment and discover which approaches come most naturally to you. Explore new possibilities and learn to master what was formerly difficult or even impossible.

ANTOINE MESMER,

Docteur en Medecine,

De la Faculté de Vienne, en Autriche

Anton Mesmer
Courtesy Bibliotheque Nationale

LE BACQUET DE M. MESMER,
ou Représentation fidelle des Opérations du Magnetisme Animal.

Mesmer Conducting A Bacquet
Courtesy Bibliotheque Nationale

Pierre Janet
Courtesy of Bibliotheque Nationale

Jean Martin Charcot
Courtesy of Bibliotheque Nationale

Emile Coué

Coue with His Patients in His Garden

Milton H. Erickson

Ernest Rossi

Jerome D. Frank

Josephine and Ernest Hilgard

PART TWO

The Pillars of Hypnosis

T he inner mind is the foundation of self hypnosis. On this foundation, the pillars of hypnosis rest: the unconscious, the interaction between mind and body, and suggestion. Use these pillars for building the skills of hypnosis.

Three

The Unconscious

Like the empty sky it has no boundaries
Yet it is right in this place, ever profound and clear
When you seek to know it, you cannot see it
You cannot take hold of it

But you cannot lose it
In not being able to get it you get it
When you are silent, it speaks

When you speak, it is silent
The great gate is wide open to bestow alms
And no crowd is blocking the way.

-- Zen Koan, *Mumonkan*

The unconscious holds a certain fascination, mysterious and undefinable, always transcending our rational explanations. Hypnosis allows us to draw from our unconscious potential even if we do not understand everything about it. From the pragmatic perspective, truth arises from use, so we develop our unconscious capacities as we continue to explore their use more deeply.

Unconscious Intelligence

The conscious employs aware, deliberate thinking, but the unconscious involves aspects of cognitive processing that lie outside awareness. The unconscious has its own intelligence and logic that takes in information, thinks, and can draw conclusions through inference. This processing does not necessarilly follow sequential logic. Milton Erickson used the example of solving a problem. Consciously we might reason in a sequence from A to B to C to D to find solutions to a problem. But unconsciously, we can make intuitive leaps, from understanding to understanding, without knowing the basis or logical steps. Sometimes, the steps to the answer remain unclear. Other times they may be found by backtracking, from D to A. We do not experience unconscious processing itself, but do perceive the consequences resulting from unconscious thinking--intuitive insights.

The unconscious is not merely a repository of repressed conflicts from the conscious mind, as described in some analytical models. Nor is it simply primitive primary processing. The unconscious can be a reservoir of positive potential, not merely the negative repository. The unconscious may contain conflicts and include primary processing, but reaches towards higher and better integration. There is an individualized, intelligently oriented sophistication to unconscious processing. The unconscious has many facets. Sensitizing yourself to its subtlety is a key to building self hypnotic skills.

Unconscious as Intuition

Intuition expresses the poetry of the unconscious. Jung characterized intuition as the psychological function that transmits perceptions in an unconscious way. (Berne 1977, 4)

THE UNCONSCIOUS

Intuitive processing is intelligent, pathway to truth and higher consciousness. Intuition is valuable to develop.

Aristotle believed intuitive functioning is an extremely sophisticated process, based on our ability to sense and perceive at a basic level. At the next level of cognition above intuition, we can retain sense perception. We know that we perceive. At a still higher level, we systematize such memories. Aristotle recognized intuition intelligently synthesizes data. Since this occurs outside of awareness, people know something without knowing how they know it. Synthetic unconscious processing occurs without conscious recognition of how it happens. "To the rationally minded, mental processes appear to work backward. His conclusions are reached before the premises" (Berne 1977, 149).

People experience uncanny hunches, spontaneous familiarity, or insightful realizations. Intuitive truth is usually recognized, not learned. Most people are aware of having intuitions. Some rely on them. Intuitions may be extremely clear for some people, vague to others. Intuitions involve sensitivity to nonverbal, nonrational phenomena. Some believe this sensitivity is a more accurate way of knowing reality's truth. Self hypnosis evokes the use of intuitive mental faculties, permitting them to develop.

Whether intuition is more perceptive than rational awareness is not the issue here. Both consciousness, through awareness and rationality, and unconsciousness, through intuition and unconscious experiencing, are important. Jung saw this when he said:

Conscious and unconscious do not make a whole when one of them is suppressed and injured by the other. If they must contend, let it at least be a fair fight with equal rights on both sides; Both are aspects of life...It is the old game of hammer and anvil: between them the patient iron is forged into an indestructible whole, an individual. (Jung 1981, 283)

Everyday, Out of Awareness Phenomena

The unconscious is continually active during everyday life. For example, as you read the words on this page, you are probably not aware of your foot. But now that "foot" is mentioned you might notice that yours is cold or warm, light or heavy or perhaps feels tingly. As your attention turns there, you can perceive your foot experience. Sensation in your foot was always present, but when thoughts were directed elsewhere these feelings were unconscious. Attention mediates your perception, but the experience exists whether consciously perceived or not. Unconscious perception is similar to the old philosophical question: If a tree falls in a forest and no one is there to hear it, does it make a sound? People can have experiences with thoughts about the experience, but be unaware of them. This does not mean that these experiences do not occur since they can be recalled later. The experience is unconscious.

Consciousness registers a multitude of experiences at once. Cognitive psychology researchers have found that our immediate short term memory cannot exceed seven plus or minus two bits of information at one time. (Miller, 1956) Anything beyond this goes unnoticed consciously, but research shows that it may be registered unconsciously. The unconscious continually absorbs much more information than consciousness perceives at any given moment. This ability is used when a witness to a crime is hypnotized to recall details of the event. The witness might feel unable to remember certain specifics, such as a license number, but under hypnosis the entire scene can be recreated as a vivid hallucination. Although there can be errors in trance recollection, the memory can also be accurate. The witness searches in trance to see the license number as if watching a movie replay. Information can be perceived and stored unconsciously, outside of awareness. Retrieval may be possible under hypnosis, though the recollection may also be influenced.

The unconscious retains memories, concepts and learnings experienced over the years. As children grow they learn how to walk, read, and write. With each stage of development, certain skills and abilities are mastered; earlier ones are incorporated or transformed. This requires applications of intelligence, emotional maturity, and body coordination.

Abilities are stored in the unconscious, not just as the specific, actual learned skill, but also as a more generalized potential to learn how to learn. For example, skills used to form letters of the alphabet in early childhood are taken for granted as an adult, yet those abilities will evolve further. These skills are automatically applied by the unconscious. Making lines, circles, spacings, and combinations may be applied later as an architect, an artist, or a builder. Writers focus on the ideas they are trying to express rather than the lettering used to express it, unless they are calligraphers. Forming each letter on the page takes place without thought, regulated by the unconscious.

Your unconscious has many learnings and understandings you may have applied in different contexts throughout your life. Connections can be made without conscious effort in trance.

Automatic Habits

Daily routine becomes automatic, regulated by the unconscious. The wake-up alarm goes off in the morning and we automatically shut it off. We walk so naturally and easily that we may never think about the complex links between mind and body coordinating unconsciously, unless something goes wrong, and we have a problem. Try to remember yesterday's activities. Some parts are murky and difficult to recall. But after concentration you probably reclaim more and more details as you bring automatic activities into your awareness. Lawrence Kubie explains how unconscious habits come about:

Once any such act is fully learned, it can be initiated quite independently of inner physical prodding merely by contemplating the goal. As this happens the entire constellation is triggered as a unit by the symbol which represents the goal; and we thereupon become unaware of the innumerable intermediate steps which make up the act. It is in this way that our thinking processes acquire the ability to leap over many intervening steps as we perform complex authentic processes. (Kubie 1961, 33)

Psychoanalyst Bellak distinguishes three levels of the unconscious: 1) the physiological, 2) the structural, 3) the dynamic (Bassin, 1969) The first two levels, physiological and structural, occur automatically, without conscious thought. The physiological and structural levels are not the content of psychoanalysis. Level three, the dynamic, is unawareness resulting from repressed psychological content, unacceptable to consciousness but occasionally struggling to awareness.

Psychoanalytic theory delved deeply into the third level, disregarding the first two levels of the unconscious. In so doing, a great deal of positive potential was overlooked. The approach to self hypnosis developed here draws on all three levels, but we do not believe dynamic content must be repressed.

The Unconscious as Set:
Russian Set Theory

Set theory is helpful for mapping unconscious processes. This theory offers a model for how the unconscious functions. The first two levels hold the key to understanding. The concept of unconscious repression is unnecessary. The Russian theory of set offers an alternative to the psychoanalytic "dynamic" unconscious.

In 1860 Fechner did preliminary research showing that an illusion of the estimation of weight could be produced when a subject was given a preset for the object's weight. First, subjects held an experimental object of a certain weight. Next, they held a second object, the same size and appearance, but lighter. Subjects reported the second object felt just as heavy as the first one. Fechner explained this phenomenon as motor set. Subjects expected similar looking objects would be the same weight.

Nearly a century later, Russian researcher Uznadze (1966) experimented with the boundaries of the earlier hypothesis. He found that the illusion created in Fechner's motor set experiments was not limited to motor phenomena. Uznadze expanded his research, testing whether expectancy principles applied more widely. He used alternatives to motor response such as pressure response, visual response, and auditory response. Uznadze concluded from his experiments that the phenomena of set involves a unified response, a modification of the individual personality, of the organism as a whole. This modification expresses itself in a wide variety of perceptual modes. During the control tests, he theorized, an expectancy or specific set is developed and fixed. Even though set is not consciously noticed, it is responsible for what is experienced, the basis for consequential action.

Uznadze specified two levels of mental life. First, the setting level, *sl,* is where behavior is completely conditioned. These sets control behavior and impulses out of awareness. The second level, objectification, occurs when people perceive something through the set without reacting directly to the thing itself.

Complex stimuli act on people as signals, eliciting reactions outside of conscious awareness. The separation between the objective effect of a stimulus on the one hand, and consciousness of the stimulation on the other is dissociation. (Bassin, 1969)

Dissociation occurs often in life, accounting for the automation of habits. Beginning under conscious control, a chain of behavior for a purpose gradually loses its conscious origin. Walking, writing, or driving a car are examples of activities that began with deliberate, conscious effort and attention but gradually became unconscious automatic skills after habitual practice. These actions may be performed without consciousness.

Uznadze's theory of set provides a model for understanding the complex noncognized influences that act upon a person outside of awareness. The influence of expectancy can have significant effects on the dynamics of conscious experience.

Erickson and Rossi developed their concept of the Acceptance Set or Yes Set as a way to engage cooperation and receptivity to hypnosis and suggestions. They found that when the hypnotist tried to relate to subjects through their real interests and concerns, subjects developed a positive feeling of involvement and acceptance of the process. Acceptance Set leads to an easier transition into trance. (Erickson & Rossi 1976, 58)

Trance as Unconscious Functioning

The centipede was happy, quite
Until a toad in fun
Said, "Pray, which leg goes after which?"
This worked his mind to such a pitch
He lay distracted in a ditch
Considering how to run (Watts 1957, 27).

In trance, unconscious processing flows freely with little or no interference from consciousness. Indirect forms of suggestion help to disengage consciousness, allowing unconscious thinking and problem solving to take place without interference.

Unconscious thinking tends to be without an object or content of consciousness. Edmund Husserl believed that consciousness always comprises an intention or meaning complex for all its processes. (Zaner 1970, 135) Consciousness is directed toward the world. Therapeutic unconscious processing is a gap, a creative moment, in the stream of consciousness (Rossi 1972). Everyday learnings, meanings, interpretations, and beliefs are temporarily suspended. There is no object or intended meaning for unconscious processes. In that open space, the gap, the individual can experience anew.

The unconscious is capable of functioning without just one set of fixed assumptions or meaning sense. Freed from the bonds of preconception, we have an opportunity to make new connections, leading to new potentials. Therapeutic trance bypasses limitations to brings about a healthier adjustment. Trance gives opportunities for creative moments.

Associative Qualities of the Unconscious

The unconscious cognizes in a stream of associations, a free flow of natural, active, creative processing without intervention of conscious purpose. The unconscious makes associations just outside of awareness throughout the day. This process is extremely useful in hypnosis and trance processes.

William James carefully defined and described associative principles. James believed that when two brain processes have been active at the same time or in immediate succession, one tends to excite the other. This is basis for the law of association (James 1896, 566).

Association by similarity occurs from the free flow of thoughts. Similar ideas become linked, forming compounds that link to other ideas. Seemingly dissimilar ideas can end up mentally connected.

Our musings pursue an erratic course, swerving continually into some new direction traced by the shifting play of interest as it ever falls on some partial item in each complex representation that is evoked. Thus it so often comes about that we find ourselves thinking at two nearly adjacent moments of things separated by the whole diameter of space and time. Not till we carefully recall each step of our cogitation do we see how naturally we came by Hodgson's law to pass from one to the other...this is the ordinary process of the association of ideas... (James 1896 573)

Some associative processes are influenced by learning. For example, if we mention the word swallow, ornithologists will think of birds, throat specialists will think of throat diseases, and thirsty people might realize how much they want a drink of water. Associations are also influenced by how recent, vivid, or congruent the ideas are. All in all, the process of association is complex and multi-faceted. Research is difficult since the phenomenon is outside of awareness.

Despite its complexities, the flow of unconscious associations is not random, but evolves out of a person's individuality. Patterns of association reflect our past, including likes and dislikes, conflicts and agreements, needs, actualities and expectancies. Many other external and internal experiences can be crystallized through associative metaphors.

Learning takes place in therapeutic trance. Sometimes our learning leads to an original discovery. Other times we assimilate, recombine, or restructure old understandings. New possibilities and changes follow from recombining and interspersing of meaning into the associative processes of the unconscious mind.

Dreams: Free Flow of Images

Unconscious processing has been described thus far in terms of thought. But sometimes the unconscious is manifested as images or pictures. These images often reflect deep levels of inner experience, unknown to consciousness. A single picture can encode many possible meanings and learnings. Dreams are like this. A few images can symbolize a lengthy scenario.

Dreams occur spontaneously and yet meaningfully in trance. For example, a hypnotherapy client of ours had a vivid image in trance of a woman wearing a dark shawl. Upon awakening she felt puzzled as she described her image. Therapeutic exploration brought out the connection to her Italian background and her feelings about her mother who had been sedentary and withdrawn. This client was involved in many community organizations, having decided early in her life to be different from her mother. The symbolic image brought forth associations that helped her to better understand and moderate her tendency to over-commit herself

Sometimes dream images are misleading. One client had a recurring dream of a frightening monster chasing her. Night after night she was repeatedly terrified by the dream. She was a very quiet, sweet person who always tried to be considerate, kind and warm. She rarely got angry and found such emotions difficult to accept. As she worked in therapy she began to conceive the monster not as a foreign body attacking her, but rather as her own angry feelings. She had crystallized her conflict into a symbolic image. After she accepted this, she was able to include more of her personality into her everyday life and stopped having nightmares. This symbol from her unconscious, though feared and avoided, turned out to hold the key to resolving her difficulty. The unconscious can express a complex emotional conflict in one seemingly terrifying image.

Dreams have also inspired great discoveries. Kekule's breakthrough of the benzene ring structure emerged from a dream. He was struggling day after day, trying to uncover a configuration to account for the unique properties of benzene. One night he fell asleep working on his calculations and had a very unusual, vivid dream. He saw a snake twirling around, chasing its own tail. Eventually the spinning snake caught its tail and turned as a circle. When Kekule awoke, he knew that he had solved the problem. Benzene arranges its molecules as a ring, a possibility he had previously overlooked! He returned to the data and was able to empirically show the validity of his insight, still accepted today. Kekule's unconscious synthesized the intellectual understandings into a symbol he could consciously trace back to the data. Dreams can be a source of creative ideas.

Morton Prince (1854-1926) viewed dreams as one of many altered states in which people unconsciously work out difficulties. He states:

> *Under conditions of stress, individuals have resorted to a repertoire of automatic self-healing mechanisms. The most important of these so-called altered states of consciousness, dreams, dissociated states, a variety of religious experiences. (Zeig 1982, 383)*

Our approach to self hypnosis uses this theory of dreams. Dreams symbolically express or represent our needs and concerns. People can utilize this valuable communication from their unconscious in trance to resolve difficulties and expand potential. Research has shown hypnotic hallucinations are similar in character to natural dreams, and so both are equally effective windows into the unconscious. Self hypnosis can help to tap this potential.

The Unconscious as Right Brain:
An Oversimplification

The unconscious has been defined by some as the right brain. This theory simplifies the conception of the unconscious and of hemisphericity. However, split brain theory is important in understanding the unconscious.

History of Hemisphericity Research

When the brain is looked at under a microscope, the two halves appear to be structured much the same. It is not surprising that through most of history, researchers thought the two halves of the brain functioned identically. Only in the past 100 years have the very different functions of the two hemispheres been discovered. Neurologists first recognized the left brain controls the right side of the body and the right brain controls the left. In the early years, researchers thought the left side that controls language and complex cognitive abilities was the most important side. According to Gardner:

> *The left hemisphere became the one to have, if you are having only one. Indeed, neurologists were fond of citing case reports of individuals who were born without a right hemisphere, or who had lost their entire right hemisphere in an accident or through surgery, who none-the-less coped successfully with the business of living. (Gardner 1974, 353)*

Evidence gradually emerged to indicate that the right hemisphere might be important as well. Research in England during World War II revealed that right hemisphere damaged patients were deficient in their ability to organize spatially. (Gardner, 1974) They had trouble finding their way back to their rooms on the wards. Dressing became a problem. Research revealed that the right hemisphere also played an important part in basic visual skills, depth perception, gestalt formation, and tactile or somato-sensory skills.

In the early 1960's the two halves of the brain were actually severed. This opened up a wealth of specific understandings. The first split-brain experiment was done on a cat by Ronald Meyers and Roger Sperry at the University of Chicago. They found:

Each hemisphere...has its own....private sensations, thoughts and ideas, all of which are cut off from the corresponding experiences in the opposite hemisphere. Each left and right hemisphere has its own private chain of memories and learning experiences that are inaccessible to recall by the other hemisphere. In many respects each disconnected hemisphere appears to have a separate 'mind of its own.' (Gazzaniga 1973, 257)

Though the left hemisphere controls language, the right hemisphere could be taught to communicate its rich experience by using special techniques. Researchers found that the right hemisphere has some language ability, can emote, learn, and remember without the left hemisphere knowing. Although the left hemisphere is superior in managing verbal processing of information, the right hemisphere proved superior in managing visual-spatial tasks.

More detailed research has determined that both hemispheres process language but that they accomplish it differently, verbally versus spatially. The left hemisphere sequentially transforms each letter into an internal acoustic code (i.e. names them) The right hemisphere examines all the letters simultaneously looking for variations in shape. The left is interested in semantic similarity; the right is interested in structural similarities. (Nebes, 1977) The right hemisphere organizes and processes data in terms of complex wholes, perceiving the total rather than the parts. The left hemisphere analyzes input sequentially. It abstracts out the relevant details and associates these with verbal signals. Drawings by left hemisphere damaged patients had a correct overall configuration but no detail. Right hemisphere damaged patients did drawings full of details but with no coherent organization.

Concept of the Right Brain as Unconscious

Popularized characterizations of the two brains went through a reverse of the old prejudice against the left brain. The left brain was no longer the best brain: The left was now considered slow and ineffectual for certain applications. "The classic left-brain approach to dancing is a perfect example of doing something the hard way with appalling results." (Blakeslee, 1983: 23) Blakeslee, in his book on the right brain, defined intuition as:

> *A thinking process which cannot be verbally explained, taking in large masses of data in parallel without separately considering each factor. This clearly refers to right brain functions. (Blakeslee, 1983: 25)*

He goes on to equate the unconscious with the right brain because:

THE UNCONSCIOUS

What makes the unconscious mind unconscious is the fact that, though it influences our behavior, we have difficulty in verbally explaining its actions (Blakeslee, 1983: 26).

The nonverbal memory of the right brain is not accessible to the verbal left brain, just as intuitive unconscious understandings can influence behavior without conscious awareness. From this viewpoint, we have two minds--two personalities that can be reacting very differently to the same situation.

Beyond Specialization

These concepts were based on early and incomplete findings of split brain researchers that the right brain was nonverbal and therefore not capable of conscious thought. Brain researchers Gazzaniga and LeDoux directly addressed this issue in a later book. (1978) They tested individuals whose two brain halves were severed. They found the split-brain subject to be fully capable of answering questions relating to his personal identity, his plans for the future, his likes and dislikes, even when responding from his right brain. The authors concluded:

Thus it would appear that the right hemisphere, along with but independent of the left, can possess conscious properties following brain bisection. In other words, the mechanisms of human consciousness can be split and doubled by split-brain surgery. (Gazzaniga 1978, 145)

Our own research (Simpkins & Simpkins, 1983) corroborated this. Right hemisphere-oriented people were not found to be more unconsciously capable in hypnotherapy than left hemisphere-oriented people. Paradoxically, lefts did better with hypnosis than rights, which seemed at first to contradict the view of right brain theorists. These findings revealed the complexity and variability of human processing. Categorizing the unconscious as simply nonverbal right hemisphere functioning does a disservice to the integrative capacities of the whole person. Gazzaniga and LeDoux feel that specialization theory fails to account for analysis and synthesis, important facets of the cognitive repertoire of both cerebral hemispheres. Integration is primary. Synthesis is individualized.

We still have much to learn about the differences and similarities between the two hemispheres.

Overall, we are compelled to say that attempts to reduce hemispheric differences to a simple formula have not encountered striking success; and in view of the long evolutionary history that led to the present cerebral organization, it may, after all, be rather foolish to expect a straightforward solution to this great mystery of the brain. (Gardner 1974, 382)

The brain halves can function independently or together. The integration of conscious and unconscious is the basis for working with self hypnosis as presented in this book. Just as an unconscious thought cannot be known without becoming conscious, many conscious thoughts and experiences are enhanced and colored by unconscious set, mood, preconception, and so on. Unconscious and conscious are both important.

The Assumptive World

Brain integration is intimately related to our assumptive world. People predict and anticipate events using assumptions, beliefs, attitudes, and expectations. According to Jerome D. Frank, the assumptive world is:

A shorthand expression for a highly structured, complex, interacting set of values, expectations, and images of oneself and others, which guide and in turn are guided by a person's perceptions and behavior and which are closely related to his emotional states and his feelings of well-being...The more enduring assumptions become organized into attitudes with cognitive, affective, and behavioral components. (Frank 1973, 27)

Some assumptions are unconscious, taken for granted as true, without correction from awareness. Attitudes deriving from these assumptions remain relatively stable, coloring and influencing our interactions with the environment. For example, catastrophic expectations can result in anxiety, discouragement, and an inability to handle stressful situations due to fearing the worst. This can lead to negative beliefs and assumptions about events in general. Attitudes may also be associated with positive expectancies, helping people meet difficult circumstances hopefully and confidently.

Assumptions and beliefs may be learned from the interpersonal realm of family and friends, religion, culture, and school, often without consciously evaluating. Others evolve from the intrapersonal, the interaction of one's own personality with the world. For example, most people think carefully and then choose a profession, but personal beliefs and attitudes about work are often taken for granted and unconscious. Some people believe that work is a struggle, an uncomfortable ordeal. Others see it as a temporary means to free time on weekends, something to get through with as little effort as possible. Still others treat work as personal commitment and devotion, an essential meaning for their life. Attitudes change somewhat as life passes, as well. For example, at retirement age, work has a different meaning than at twenty. These attitudes and values may have evolved from personal inner dynamics, from interpretations of the parent's way of dealing with work, or from response to outer circumstance, like a devastating war. Whatever the origins, our beliefs, values, assumptions, and sets influence the kinds of real life choices we make. Hypnosis allows us to modify our assumptive world, suspending its usual limits so we can make alterations to our benefit.

Language as Expression of the Unconscious

Through language we symbolize our interpretation of reality. Burke states that, whether we realize it or not, we are symbol-users.

But can we bring ourselves to realize just what that formula implies, just how overwhelmingly much of what we mean by 'reality' has been built up for us through nothing but our symbol systems? (Burke 1969, 5)

We derive concepts from symbols and words, simplifying reality. We conceive, then we believe. After years of habit, we may begin to mistake our symbols and concepts for the reality they are intended to point to. Then our use of language separates our personal experience from the actual reality of the complex and mutifaceted object.

> *Language referring to the realm of the nonverbal is necessarily talk about things in terms of what they are not--and in this sense we start out beset by paradox. Such language is but a set of labels, signs for helping us find our way about...such terms are sheer emptiness, as compared with the substance of the thing they name. (Burke 1969, 10)*

The unconscious lies behind and beyond symbols, words and concepts, a rich and varied nonverbal experience. When we speak spontaneously without thinking, our language may reflect unconscious meanings. The natural uncontrolled flow of words, if listened to carefully, can reveal much about our assumptive world through personal feelings and moods, as well as inner dynamics. The unconscious is expressed through the use of words as well as the spaces between words. The deeper ground of the symbol is not just a symbol. It is something more. Through the medium of language we attempt to convey reality's meaning. Yet reality always transcends conceptual boundaries.

B. L. Whorf characterized this conception of language in general:

> *Every language contains terms that have come to attain cosmic scope of reference, that crystallize in themselves the basic postulates of an unformulated philosophy, in which is couched the thoughts of a people, a culture, a*

civilization, even of an era. (Carroll 1956, 61)

These terms are taken-for-granted assumptions that help to shape people in their culture and historical context. Words like *byte* or *online* may have seemed strange to persons who lived before computers and the internet, yet the children of today take computer terminology for granted as part of their understood reality. Similarly, the parents of these children have accepted certain words, terms for television concepts, such as "channels," as a taken for granted part of reality. To their parents, television was extraordinary at first. We cannot imagine what tomorrow will be. But our children, and their children in turn, will surely take it for granted.

⌘

Intuition, habits, sets, dreams, associations, assumptions about the world, and even our use of language often occur outside awareness. The unconscious functions naturally in everyday life, always with the capability to help us return to the ground of reality to surpass our learned limitations. Now that we have familiarized ourselves with the positive potential of the unconscious, we can begin to make this unconscious potential truly useful to us.

Four

Mind & Body

I am my body only in so far as for me the body is an essentially mysterious type of reality, irreducible to those determinate formulae (no matter how interestingly complex they might be) to which it would be reducible if it could be considered merely as an object.

--Gabriel Marcel 1969

Mind and body were considered separate by the early philosophers. Descartes' famous declaration in his *Meditations*, "I think, therefore I am" set mind and body apart. Philosophers have had to answer to Descartes ever since. Cartesian philosophy was based on the theory of knowledge that we can know with certainty only through our own mind. In order to question or doubt, we must first think. Thus a thinker must exist. *Cogito, ergo sum.* The world of objects and of other people can only be proved to exist from our consciousness of them. This introduced the notion that reality is dual: mind and body, or spirit and matter. Mind cannot be understood as simply existing in physical space: It cannot be seen, measured or touched, except indirectly, by inference. Only the body exists in space, is measurable, and can be directly observed. Later discoveries would call into question Descartes' dualistic view of mind and body.

The Personal Equation

At the Greenwich Observatory in 1796 a seemingly innocuous event took place that was to change the history of astronomy and of philosophical thought for all time. Maskelyne, the *Astronomer Royal* of the observatory, fired his assistant Kinnebrook because the assistant's measurements of the star movements were eight tenths per second slower than his own. Kinnebrook had been hired to watch through the telescope as a clock ticked. He was supposed to time the star's motion from one parallel sighting wire to another. The method of measurement was usually considered to be accurate to one tenth of a second. Maskelyne thought his assistant indolent for recording such inaccurate measurements!

The significance of this event went unrecognized. But twenty-five years later an astronomer named Bessel (1784-1846) noted the same phenomenon. He was so puzzled that he sent for the complete report to investigate whether this personal difference held constant with other experienced observers. Together with another astronomer, Bessel compared individual reports and found they differed by more than a full second! The formula they worked out for the difference came to be called "The Personal Equation." Bessel believed that the delay was due to the time that mental processes take.

Later investigators developed and elaborated these findings. In 1850 a famous pioneer of experimental psychology, Hermann Helmholtz (1821-1895), claimed that impulses travel slower than sound waves. Later experiments using different methods also found variability according to personal reactions.

Many people came to believe the speed of transmission of nerve impulses was determined by variables like height. John C.

Whitehorn (1894-1971), Johns Hopkins Hospital researcher and Chief of Staff, wondered if this was true. He investigated whether tall people take longer for the standardized medical knee jerk reflex than short people. Whitehorn found no standardized significant difference, only individual differences. People's reactions are not determined in fixed ways, even though there are many common features. The personal equation was an individual one. Whitehorn extended this into his clinical work as a psychotherapist. Individual understanding is primary.

Gustav Theodor Fechner (1801-1887) was versatile: a humanist, poet, physicist, and philosopher with a mystical feeling about the unity of life. To Fechner, the whole earth was like an organism, a live, unified spiritual being he called *gaiea*. The winds were its breathing, the crust of the earth its skin, the rivers and oceans were its veins and arteries. He urged an ecological approach, far ahead of his times. Though few heeded him then, his research was groundbreaking. He wanted to show the unity of mind and body through an equation.

The relative increases of bodily energy and measure of the increase of the corresponding mental intensity could be mathematically computed as a ratio between the two.
(Boring 1950, 280)

Fechner is known scientifically for psychophysics, which he explained in his text, the *Elemente der Psychophysik*. He believed that psychophysics was the exact science of the fundamental relations of dependency between the mind and body.

Reaction times to measurement efforts vary not only according to the personal equation, but also differ with the set or expectation of the observer. Expectant attitudes predispose an observer to react slower or faster, depending on how the expectancies are sequenced.

Expectancy and the Mind-Body Interaction

Expectancy or set theory was an important concept in psychology for many years. Fechner demonstrated that muscles can be given a set which then persists in judging how heavy something is. (See Chapter 3) Fechner showed that once an expectation that a weight of a certain size looks a certain way is given to the muscles, another identical looking weight will usually be estimated to weigh the same, even if in actuality it is heavier or lighter. Russian psychologists went farther. Psychology developed in Russia was based in creating expectant sets toward certain actions and perceptions. Sets or expectations can be given in all of the possible modalities.

Placebo research has shown that expectation and set link the mind and body. Placebos are inert substances containing no active ingredients of any kind. In early placebo studies, a control group was given placebos. They believed the placebo contained medicine that would help their condition. These subjects often improved as much as the group who received real medicine. Researchers learned from these studies that the positive expectation of help influenced the physiological condition toward health.

Researchers developed these concepts further, conducting experiments utilizing pure placebo response. In one experiment (Park and Covi, 1965, in Frank et. al., 1978) experimenters told their subjects, "We are giving you a placebo. That means the pill is completely inert. However, many people have been helped by placebos, and we believe it will help you too." Most participating subjects gained dramatic relief from their problems. Some even requested refills! This unexpected finding was disregarded at first, but was later confirmed by other research. (Frank, 1991)

The placebo effect is now well accepted today. Comparison with placebo is an indispensible part of clinical trial testing for modern medicines. Only if the drug works significantly better than a placebo is it confirmed as effective for treatment.

The influence of the imagination over the body can over-shadow the action of a medication. In one study, subjects were given warm milk containing a medication that is a powerful stimulant. Subjects were told that the warm milk was soothing and usually produced sleep: it did!

These experiments illustrate the powerful interaction between mind and body. Even after many years of experiments, how this occurs is still not clearly understood. The mind's effect on the body should be recognized, accepted and used in treatment. The mind need not always dominate the body to be helpful, nor does the body have to dominate the mind. They can interrelate in a harmonious manner.

Directing attention to physiological responses can be very useful at times. Meditation is gaining wide acceptance as a method of using mental training to help bring about inner calm and a feeling of well being. For example, people can deliberately cultivate relaxation to reduce their stress response, helping to heal an ulcer condition. Calm relaxation has been used to help lower blood pressure. Controlled research using hypnosis, biofeedback, relaxation training, and meditation have all indicated there is good reason to accept useful links between mind and body. Correct technique can make higher potentials of functioning available. (Simpkins & Simpkins, 1996, 1997, 1998)

Mind-Body Interaction

That the relation of people to their society and to the people around them can influence the incidence, the prevalence, the course, and the mortality of diseases seems clear enough. The questions at issue are the questions of when they do so, under what circumstances, by what mechanisms, and to what extent. (Hinkle 1973, 47)

Frank stated that anxiety and depression, the most frequent symptoms of patients in psychotherapy, are direct expressions of demoralization. (Frank 1973, 271) Frank showed the importance of hope in many articles and books:

Efforts to heighten the patient's positive expectations may be as genuinely therapeutic as free association or habit training. (Frank 1965, 385)

Herbert Benson (1979) illustrated the effects of negative attitudes in the extreme case of voodoo death. He described documented instances of voodoo death as a real phenomenon, mediated by attitudes of hopelessness and certainty that escape is impossible. Residents of islands such as Haiti, Jamaica, or even the Bahamas may have heard or seen instances of voodoo curses, with dire consequences following for the recipient. A shared assumptive world of beliefs and attitudes about the power of voodoo contributes to its devastating effects. Locals know curse symbols. When a curse is cast, there is fertile ground for the mechanism of self suggestion to bring about the feared event. Voodoo shows the important role the mind plays.

How can thoughts and experiences that seem to be in the mind be brought to the level of the body? How can the mind-body gap be bridged, when negative expectancy interferes? Hypnosis works with both mind and body to help bridge the gap.

Gestalt Therapy: A Theory of Mind-Body Unity

Gestalt Therapy, founded by Frederick S. Perls, treated Descartes' mind-body split as a symptom of neurosis, due to defensive alienation. Perls believed mind and body should not be separated, they should interrelate in a pattern or unity, a gestalt. Mind is embodied in each individual's unique organism, in relationship to his or her environment. The point of contact and natural identification is the boundary where interaction takes place. When people have conflict and consequent tension, they tend to identify themselves with one part of their conflict and alienate themselves from the other. Which part they identify with depends on their need, sense of identity, and the demands of the situation. For example, if you are sitting in class, you probably will be more identified with your mind by ideas and concepts. Body concerns are background unless an urgent need or interest begins to draw your attention. If a throbbing headache comes on, it draws your attention away from the learning situation. Suddenly body awareness becomes central until you manage to either take care of what is bringing on the pain or else stoically accept it as you keep your attention on the teacher. Awareness of body sensations is a built-in part of the signaling system to remind us to attend to what we need. This can start the motor for action, encouraging us to do something about our needs. By getting in touch you begin to find a healthy, motivated, creative adjustment. But Perls thought contact had to be conscious and aware. Hypnosis and meditation demonstrate that contact and orientation do not need to be conscious. Individuals vary in this.

Sometimes we must dissociate our body concern temporarily from awareness in order to accomplish our goals. For example, in 1988 during an important soccer match, a number of players vital to the the San Diego Sockers team were injured. They gave themselves to the team effort anyway for the decisive final game to try to win the championship. The goal of winning was most important to them at that time. Concerns about body pain and discomfort became background to their commitment to victory. The players temporarily surpassed the limitations posed by their injuries.

Gestalt Therapy views body awareness as our primary experience of being-in-the-world. Perls often said, "I am my body." Clients learn to concentrate on body sensations and take responsibility for any experienced tensions. In this method, awareness is curative.

A body awareness technique originally used in early Gestalt Therapy (Perls, Hefferline, Goodman 1951), is characteristically used to get in touch, to increase awareness. You can experiment with this in the following exercise.

Body Focusing

First describe to yourself what you are experiencing. Pay close attention to the sensations there. Wait for a fantasy or train of thoughts, feelings, and ideas associated with it. For example, you might have an image of being in a tense social situation that you handled with restraint in spite of feeling annoyed. Intuitions and ideas about what things mean can pop into your mind. With practice, you learn to note and observe carefully what emerges.

The body speaks in its own symbolic language, communicating through posture, gesture, and movement. In Gestalt Therapy, the therapist observes the body language of patients while they sit and talk. Then the therapist interrupts the patients' defensive verbalizing, and requests that they express in descriptive words what their posture and gesture really intend. The body does not lie. Patients learn to expand their perception of deeper feelings, attitudes, thoughts, getting in touch. As they express the meaning indicated by their gesture or posture, they gain self awareness, and reclaim their inner resources to resolve conflicts. This method depends on awareness to evoke change.

Homeostasis is the natural tendency of the body to seek equilibrium, balance, and rest. This well-accepted physiological theory holds for the personality as well. We experience tension when a need emerges and becomes urgent. The need tends to organize corresponding behavior, a pattern of action required to satisfy and balance the deficit. For example, when we need water, we feel thirsty and notice potential sources of water. Thoughts, images, and impulses that are oriented around water come to mind. Eventually, we seek liquid to quench our thirst, which fills the deficit. This resolves the tension, bringing completion, a unity of pattern, closure of the gestalt. Then the organism returns to a neutral balance state of "creative indifference." (Perls, 1969b) A new, more urgent need emerges and organizes a new gestalt, beginning the cycle again. People can get in touch with what they really need through self awareness, feeling and becoming conscious of their impulses, fantasies, tensions, and discomforts. Body sensations and perceptions can function as feedback signals for attuning to what is most important. But through hypnosis people can respond automatically and unconsciously to their needs, intuitively sensitized. Trust your unconscious.

Wisdom is already present, wired in. Conscious awareness is secondary. Attempts to deliberately control ourselves may interfere with the organism's built-in ability to balance itself instinctively, through satisfying needs and completing unresolved business. Self regulation is a natural characteristic of healthy life. Body and mind should be an integrated unity in health. A dualistic split between mind and body points to the problem through symbols and body language.

Become more sensitive to your body. This skill is helpful for self hypnosis since you will sometimes want to recognize minute cues from your body in trance. Hypnosis works with mind and body as a unity. Thought is reflected in body experience, and experiences of body sensations can be reflected in thoughts.

Exercise in Body Perception

Lie flat on the floor. Draw your knees up so that the soles of your feet are flat on the floor. Let your body relax, and release all unnecessary tensions. As you permit your attention to wander about and scan your body, tensions in one area may become more evident, while other areas of body sensations become background. For example, you might feel tightness in your back or shoulders now, even though you had not noticed it earlier. When you pay attention to it to let go of the tension, you might have a fantasy or a memory about an annoying situation that took place during the day. Continue to concentrate on whatever spontaneously attracts your attention. This is the essence of awareness technique: blending concentration with what spontaneously attracts your attention. It is easy to go from here to inviting the back tensions to let go as much as possible (to continue with our example), along with your concerns about it.

Your body can tell you a great deal about your deeper feelings and intuitions. There is a subtle art to attuning to this information and using it wisely. Einstein is famous for utilizing his body sensations intuitively to help him discover relativity. He believed that relativity existed because of what he felt in his body. These sensations caused him to work backwards mathematically to prove that his intuitions were true. Detectives are able to discover things because they have a hunch or feeling about it. Jazz musician Miles Davis spoke of using his body sensations to develop creative patterns for his musical compositions. These are all examples of body-mind links being used for positive goals.

Sensory Awareness

Sensory awareness, as developed by Charles Brooks and Charlotte Selver, approaches mind and body from another angle. Problems in the mind clear up when we simply pay attention to sensations without adding to them. Practitioners of this art carefully concentrate on the details of sensory experience. Thoughts become background. Instead, they focus on kinesthetic sensations such as touch, movement, relaxation, tension, weight, and breathing. People find their lives markedly enriched as chronic tensions, psychosomatic problems and character disorders ease. Therapy is facilitated when clients learn to experience without interference from thoughts. Focusing attention brings about relaxation naturally.. Sensory awareness can also be developed in everyday activities. Selver and Brooks often had students experiment with walking, sitting, and even such everyday activities as washing dishes. You can experiment with exercises to further enhance your sensory awareness

Sensory Awareness

To develop your awareness of sensations for hypnosis, this exercise is best done in the shower or bath. Begin by running the water at your usual temperature. Feel the water as it hits your body. After a few minutes turn the water to a slightly warmer temperature. Notice how this affects the sensations in your skin, whether your muscles relax, and any other feelings you might have in your body. Next, turn the water down to a cooler temperature and pay attention to these sensations. Compare how you feel now with how you felt when the water was warmer. Do not make the water too hot or too cold for comfort.

Sensory Awareness of Breathing

Sit or lie down in a comfortable position. Scan through your body with your attention, without changing anything. Simply notice what you experience. Sense your breathing. Is it easy? Labored? Slow? Quick? After awhile try to relax your breathing. Sometimes you can place your hands lightly on your rib cage and feel the rise and fall of your chest with each breath. In this approach, as in hypnosis, you do not try to deliberately change your breathing; rather, you allow the change to take place naturally. Can you allow your whole ribcage to take part in your breathing? Can you permit your abdomen to relax and move with your breathing? Can you feel your lower back and waist move? Your shoulders?

Body Therapies

Releasing body energy is important in many therapies. For example, bioenergetics, based in the ideas of Wilhelm Reich, and later evolved by Alexander Lowen, held that conflicts are represented and can be expressed symbolically in the body. Conflicts may be expressed as postural problems, chronic tensions, body image concerns or dissociated experiences of the body.

Personality tendencies are characteristically communicated unconsciously in meanings that involve the body. For example, conflicts with patterns of anxiety may be expressed in such ways as functional blindness or paralysis. These patients feel as if they are unable to see or move even though there is no physical reason for the problem. Obsessive-compulsives tend to be more oriented around thinking and do not notice their bodies. Bipolar patients often have exaggerated poorly defined body boundaries. Schizophrenics may not recognize their own body image in a mirror. Sometimes they have fluctuating hallucinatory images of their bodies.

Body therapists believe that the cure for neurosis is through corrective experiences of the integrity of the body image with emotion. The mind will follow. Therapeutic procedures may involve taking on certain postures or movements expected to help release emotions. Massage that breaks up connective tissue, like

Rolfing, is used to release blocks and free patients from conflicts symbolized structurally in tissue changes such as chronic tension. Massage gives clients access to previously repressed emotions to work through using abreaction and analysis.

Body-oriented therapies have shown that there is a close interaction between body, emotions, and thoughts. Learning to be relaxed can often help with tense attitudes. Focus on body experiencing also permits its use as a symbol system to help understand and resolve conflicts nonverbally.

Body image is the term psychologists use to refer to attitudes, beliefs, and experiences we have about our bodies.. Extensive research by Fisher (1970) indicated that character traits are associated with certain patterns of focus of attention. Body image focus varies symbolically with traits of personality. There are also characteristic distortions of body perception associated in general with specific emotions and attitudes. Thus, for example, if you are unconsciously angry at yourself, you may perceive your body as unattractive.

Body image can be helpful and positive at times. But problems often interfere with accurate experiencing of the body. Hypnosis works with both the mind and body, thereby approaching problems on a number of levels at the same time.

Ideomotor Phenomena:
Communication with Your Unconscious Mind

Hypnosis has a pragmatic solution to Descartes' mind-body split: reflex ideomotor phenomena. This occurs naturally when thought, image, or experience is automatically translated into body experience, movement, or sensation. There is no actual separation: thought becomes action, image becomes motor response, imaginary sensory experience becomes actual sensory phenomena.

In deep trance, the unconscious reinterprets sensory and motor phenomena into fantasies, hallucinations, dreams and other symbolic expressions that compound many potential meanings. Careful observation of such phenomena can be very helpful in self therapy.

Erickson and Rossi used ideomotor phenomena as doorways to other phenomena and abilities. An early paper of Erickson's, the "My Friend John Technique" explored ideomotor phenomena for trance and suggestion (Erickson, in Erickson & Rossi, 1980). Using anecdotes and theory, Erickson described how vividly imagined experiences assist people to tap into their own potentials for trance experience. By utilizing the spontaneous talents a person may have to clearly visualize someone else going into trance, a thread is spun leading to the observer's own trance. This kind of effect is natural and often surprising when it happens. It was implicit in Bernheim's work on the ideomotor phenomena centuries ago.

The simplest way to understand ideomotor phenomena is to experiment with it. The following exercise gives you an experiential sense of the conscious-unconscious, mind-body interaction.

Exercise in Ideomotor Effect: Chevreul's Pendulum

Take a plumb bob, easily procured at most hardware stores, or else use a heavy object, like a locket, a ring, or a fairly large machine nut. Hang the object from a string. Draw a large pattern on a standard piece of paper, of a

87

cross at right angles. Sit on a chair with both feet flat on the floor. Place the paper on the floor beneath you, as you rest your elbow on your knee and hold the weighted string above the paper without letting the weight touch the paper. Close your eyes. Imagine the weight swinging along one of the axis on your paper. Vividly picture it swinging, either side to side or front to back. Imagine that the swings get bigger and bigger. Open your eyes to see it swinging. Next, close your eyes again and picture the pendulum changing direction, or swinging in a circle. Do not force it to move, nor should you will it to swing. Imagine the swinging as vividly as possible, and wait for your response.

Some people might find that the movement begins very small. Others discover the pendulum seems to take off with a great deal of intensity. The effect evolves as you practice. Small movements begin to increase. Then, communicating with your unconscious becomes possible. This skill will be used later in the book to enhance your inner communication. But first accept and get in touch with your inner wisdom.

Questioning Your Unconscious Mind

You can ask questions of your inner mind and get *yes*, *no*, or *maybe* replies. Assign *no* to the horizontal axis and *yes* to the vertical. *Maybe* could be represented by circling. After you have presented a question to yourself, repeat what you did in the exercise above. The pendulum moves in a particular direction, giving an unconscious answer. Allow spontaneous response, without interfering.

Given more energy, thoughts become action as the patterns of activity shift from the fantasy potential level to the actuality level (Perls, 1969b). Freud's early theory of complexes, repressed ideas, and conflicting impulses may be understood as a logical extension of the ideomotor theory of hypnosis. The level of energy tends to determine whether thoughts remain just thoughts, or become actions, and whether actions, in turn, can lead to related thoughts.

Method actors use this to produce an emotion when they need it. Performing an associated action helps to conjure up a feeling. For example, gesturing with a clenched fist can bring up an angry feeling from deep within for a trained actor. Similarly catharsis may take place from imaginatively revisiting, feeling, and going through the personal meaning of a situation that is deeply significant. Highly stimulating memories and associated ideas tend to encourage corresponding responsive action for resolution. For example, in a scene from his videotape entitled *Grief and Pseudogrief*, Perls helped a patient feel her grief and recall her memories in detail. By accepting and feeling her grief deeply over and over again in the therapeutic interaction, she came to terms with it and began to perceive other meanings in her traumatic experience that she had not incorporated. The meaning of her grief changed, releasing her to grow and develop.

Explore ideomotor and ideosensory suggestions to perceive the unconscious link between mind and body, using your imagination. Freedom from redundant patterns of assumption becomes possible as changes in meaning take place. These useful skills will be explored and developed in the chapters to follow.

⌘

This chapter focused on integrating awareness of body and mind to open a pathway to healthy functioning. Using self hypnosis, mind and body may be coordinated in many ways. Be open to the sense data you gain from body awareness exercises. Temporarily set aside, for the purpose of personal exploration and development, any preconceptions of what your body is really like. Concentrate instead on actual experience. A new, more accurate and positive body sense becomes possible, unifying mind and body. The creative application of exercises throughout the book can help you develop this.

Five

Suggestion: Direct, Indirect,

and Beyond

Fix your thought closely on what is being said, and let your mind enter fully into what is being done, and into what is doing it.

--Marcus Aurelius

Suggestion is defined in Webster's Dictionary as the process through which an idea is brought to the mind because of its connection or association with an idea already in mind. The dictionary's second definition states that in psychology, suggestion is the inducing of an idea, decision, etc. by means of a verbal or other stimulus, in another individual who accepts it uncritically, as in hypnosis (*Webster's New World Dictionary*, 1964).

Both definitions are part of the use of suggestion in hypnosis. The dictionary definitions indicate that suggestion is more concerned with process than content. People often attempt to use self suggestion consciously, directly emphasizing the content, what they want to suggest. This can result in activating conscious rather than unconscious processes, interfering with effective therapy. Through emphasizing the process rather than the

91

content of suggestion, individualized unconscious responses are activated. This encourages and permits creative spontaneity, an important force for change.

Suggestion is an important tool of self hypnosis. It is often used in conjunction with trance, but the two are separate. Both are useful for self-directed change. Suggestion can be effectively given to yourself, in the form of self-suggestion. Coué favored self-suggestion. He helped patients, while freeing them from dependency on an external influence.

Of all the questions which arise, the most urgent from the viewpoint of the average man seems to be this--is a suggester necessary? Must one submit oneself to the influence of some other person, or can one in the privacy of one's own chamber exercise with equal success this potent instrument of health? (Coué 1923, 42)

Coué believed all suggestion is autosuggestion. Your unconscious must accept the suggestion, whether presented by your own mind, by circumstance, or by another person. Others cannot influence you without your cooperation.

Autosuggestion consists of receiving an idea and then translating it into action. Both of these operations are performed outside of awareness, unconsciously. Whether the original idea comes from within the individual or from outside by another makes no difference.

In both cases it undergoes the same process: it is submitted to the unconscious, accepted or rejected, and so either realized or ignored. (Brooks 1982, 55)

After the unconscious fully accepts it, the idea naturally tends to be brought about. Coué believed imagination is stronger than will. Once accepted, suggestion stimulates imagination. This is how the walls of will and resistance can be overcome.

Your conscious mind need not impose ideas upon your unconscious to be effective. Domination is not the essence of suggestion. Conscious and unconscious can interrelate to make positive creative adjustments possible. Suggestion uses the links between psychological and physiological levels.

Understanding suggestion requires recognition of the subtleties of conscious and unconscious processing. The main emphasis of this book is self hypnosis. Therefore, we deal primarily with auto-suggestion, suggestions that are given to yourself. This will permit you to use suggestion in positive ways.

Experiment with the ideas and exercises presented in order to personally experience how to use suggestion. Theory has a different meaning when you experience it for yourself. Unlike other disciplines, hypnosis and suggestion are more understandable when felt. Exercises in suggestion help familiarize you with your own individual parameters of suggestibility, especially useful when combined with trance.

Preparing for Suggestion:
Indirect Associative Focusing

You can enhance your ability to take suggestions through indirect associative focusing. If you permit your associations to wander aimlessly, they will not simply wander into empty space, dissociating without direction. Patterns naturally tend to direct the flow of associations. Flows of associations can be used to help link up with unconscious patterns of therapeutic importance. Contemplating associated meanings, you learn to elicit certain wished-for responses, without manipulating yourself mechanically like a puppet. In the process, you warm up for the next experience. Each experience prepares you for the next in a continuous, linked chain.

Indirect focusing uses vague energized meanings, attitudes, ideas, and experiences, somewhat similar to meditation. The experiential environment you create can make it more likely that a certain response will occur. Natural reflexes and intuitions can guide the exploration of meaningful patterns. These meanderings may be very productive.

Focusing on meaningful ideas and associations gradually mobilizes expectancies through imagination. Contact with your inner wellsprings becomes resources that are available when you explore in trance with indirect associative focusing.

Exercise in Indirect Associative Focusing

Sit quietly and close your eyes. Contemplate suggestion and self hypnosis. Can you recall times when you may have seen people hypnotized and remember ideas you have had about it? Perhaps you have only read about hypnosis. Think about what you expect will happen. Let your thoughts meander around hypnosis and suggestion. Allow yourself to warm up to the process by contemplating the possibilities.

Forms of Suggestion

Suggestion is a natural part of our daily experience. Most people simply do not know how to use it in a positive way.

SUGGESTION: DIRECT, INDIRECT, AND BEYOND

Suggestion takes many forms. Some are obvious and direct, others are subtle and barely noticeable. You can explore by experimenting with many forms of suggestion that follow.

Spontaneous and Induced Suggestion

Baudouin distinguished between spontaneous and induced suggestions. Spontaneous suggestions are occasional, involuntary responses to a stimulus as a suggestion. By contrast, induced suggestion occurs when you deliberately set yourself, using the techniques of suggestion, to have an experience or accomplish a selected goal. Another way to think of these two phenomena is as conditioning. (See Pavlov, Chapter 2 & 8) A spontaneous suggestion is like an unconditioned reflex reaction that happens automatically, reflexively. An induced suggestion can be viewed somewhat like a conditioned response where learned links are used to help accomplish goals.

Noticing Suggestive Qualities

Think of a time in your life when you sat around a camp fire, watching the dancing flames, and listening with ever increasing fascination to a terrifying tale of ghosts and spirits. Later, as you ventured back to your sleeping quarters, sounds had an eerie tone, shadows appeared to move, giving you a feeling of fear and foreboding. In this example, an idea and fantasy presented to you became a reality for you. You felt as if you were in the midst of apparitions, even if only for a few moments. For another instance, think of a time when you might have been feeling a bit depressed. You met up with a good friend whose pleasant smile and cheery disposition seemed to magically lift you from your doldrums. In this friend's presence your own thoughts and feelings seemed unnecessarily glum. Suddenly you felt positive again. You were released from your negative mood. You may recall examples of your own.

A sensation can give rise to a suggestion by interacting with a previous idea. For example, if we expect someone to visit, a pet playing in its cage may seem to sound like the ring of the doorbell. If your imagination is active enough, you may hear the telephone ring when the house is essentially silent. Ideas and expectations can bring about a spontaneous suggestion.

We interpret our sensations in part through our assumptive world. Experiences, ideas, and emotions may be suggested, as a consequence. For example, even though there is no obvious emotional meaning connected to eating, some people often want to eat when they feel a certain way. They may unintentionally have eating suggested by certain cues like anger or frustration. The action of eating is not, in this instance, just a simple response to hunger.

Personal Spontaneous Suggestion

Learning to be aware of spontaneous suggestion can be as helpful as working with the induced type. First, cultivate awareness of spontaneous suggestions, noting and observing them as they occur. Concentrate on the experience as it happens. This requires careful observation. Notice the sensory or intellectual modalities that are typically suggestive to you. As you become more aware of them, you will learn more about yourself. For example, the sounds of someone in the kitchen can suggest dinner or perhaps awakening in the morning. The smell of food can suggest its taste and the wish to eat. People with a cigarette habit often find the smell of cigarette smoke suggests to them to have a cigarette. If they successfully give up the habit, smoking is no longer suggested by smelling cigarette smoke. You may respond to spontaneous suggestion in many ways. Your personal characteristic variations are important for observing your own patterns of response. You can generalize to understanding more complex suggestive links.

Induced suggestions are given deliberately to bring about an effect. These types of suggestions can be indirect and general or direct and specific.

According to Brooks, an Englishman who studied intensively with Coué, ideas become a reality by means of *acceptation*, being fully accepted by the unconscious (Brooks 1981). A reflex response takes place which transforms ideas automatically into action. This responsiveness is integral to the mind. Induced auto-suggestion simply implies directing this entirely natural process, so the mechanisms of mind tend to bring the suggestion about. Acceptation is strongest when the conscious tides are lowest. Then unconscious associations are most likely to flow. Jung believed the threshold between conscious and unconscious lowers at times, allowing concentration to take place effortlessly and attention to be focused through involuntary processes. At such times, induced suggestion can be very effective. Jung found this phenomenon was helpful for enhancing therapy. The many types of suggestions that follow are the induced type.

Suggestion as Focused Attention

Braid considered concentration of attention to be essential for successful hypnosis and a prerequisite for the acceptance of suggestions. By narrowing your attention, suggestions are met with little or no competition from other alternatives. This approach to suggestion tends to view hypnosis as a state of focused attention that greatly facilitates responsive suggestibility.

Fixation of Attention on an Object of Interest

If you would like to experiment with this approach, find a sensory experience that has the natural quality of fascination, such as glowing coals in a fireplace, a full moon over a body of water, a quiet field in the evening, or some other stimulating scene. Let your attention be drawn exclusively to it. Ensure that you have no external demands requiring attention, and can be undisturbed as you watch. Permit your thoughts to dwell on nothing but the coals, the fire, the moon, or whatever you have chosen. In time you may have an experience of drifting into a state of deep absorption. At this point you can experiment with self-suggestion. Suggest that you see an image in the coals, or patterns on the water, etc. Try inviting such phenomena as relaxation of your arms and legs or perhaps all your muscles while you watch. You might suggest heaviness, lightness, warmth in your arms or legs, coolness in your forehead and so on. Each successful response to self suggestion tends to reinforce the general tendency of responsiveness.

Fixation on Eye Closure

In this classic exercise used by Braid, fixate your attention by looking upward until your eyes become tired. Then give yourself the suggestion: "My eyes are becoming heavy and want to close." Often the eyes water as they begin to close. Wait for your response. Follow and appreciate the individuality you might manifest in the situation. You can learn about yourself by observing your tendencies. If you find yourself somewhat unwilling or unable to open your eyes, you have gotten in touch with an involuntary level of response to suggestion. Some may experience this, others may not. With a further suggestion you can release your eyelid muscles such as, "Soon I will once again be able to open my eyes." Rest a moment, then stretch and reorient, awake and refreshed.

Suggestion as Ideomotor Phenomena

Bernheim, who popularized hypnosis as suggestion (See Chapter 1) viewed suggestion somewhat differently from fixation or auto-suggestion theories. His view of suggestion involved ideomotor action. This reflex action is not dependent on outer conditions. There are many automatically occurring mind-body interactions that can be used to bring about changes.

Ideomotor Response to Suggestion

Close your eyes and think about a tart lemon. Imagine this as vividly as possible. If your mouth begins to water, you have experienced the effects of a suggestion automatically taking place through ideomotor action.

Further Differentiation of Suggestion:
Direct, Indirect, Efferent, Afferent, Immediate, Mediate

Sidis (1898) was one of the first theorists to clearly specify a distinction between direct and indirect suggestion. Direct suggestion occurs when a hypnotist tells the subject exactly what he or she is to experience and the subject experiences this. An example of direct suggestion is "You will feel warm." Rossi states a similar conception: "Direct suggestion, by contrast, presents subjects with a stimulus that identifies what the results should be" (Erickson, Rossi, Rossi 1976, 268).

Suggestions can also be given in a subtle manner. These forms of suggestion are known as indirect suggestion. An example of an indirect suggestion is, "Would your unconscious like to experience an alteration in temperature?" Here the subject is not told exactly what to experience. The response could be warmth or coolness. Indirect suggestions are very helpful for the self hypnosis approach used in this book. The section below describes indirect suggestions in depth.

Indirect suggestions are not always given with words. Sidis pointed out that nonverbal communication can also be suggestive in an indirect way.

Instead of openly telling the subject what he should do, the experimenter produces some object or makes a movement, a gesture, which in their own silent fashion tell the subject what to do. (Sidis 1898, 19)

He further distinguished between what he called the "afferent" and the "efferent" side of suggestion:

SUGGESTION: DIRECT, INDIRECT, AND BEYOND

... Suggestion, on the one hand, with the impression of the suggested idea on the mind and its acceptance by consciousness; this is the afferent, sensory side of suggestion; and, on the other hand, with the realization of the accepted idea; this is the efferent, motor side of suggestion. (Sidis 1898, 21)

The afferent is the sensory receptive side of suggestion. The efferent side involves actually carrying out the suggestion through some physiological effect, motor action. Thus, suggestion always consist of two parts: a sensory experience and a motor action. Modern neuropsychology would confirm that sensory experience is intimately interrelated to motor response through a complex interaction in the brain.

Sidis further divided the efferent, action side, into either immediate or mediate.

In short, when there is a full and complete realization of the idea or order suggested, directly or indirectly, we have that kind of suggestion which I designate as immediate...Instead, however, of immediately taking the hint and fully carrying it into execution, the subject may realize something else, either what is closely allied with the idea suggested or what is connected with it by association or contiguity. (Sidis 1898, 22)

Thus, in the mediate response, the subject may not obey the exact suggestion explicitly as given but will carry out something similar. For example, the hypnotist might suggest that upon awakening the subject will pick up a book from the table. Instead, the subject takes the pencil sitting nearby. Mediate, open-ended responding to suggestion permits creative utilization of the subject's individuality. Sidis believed people always respond, in one way or another, to suggestions that are given. They may not do exactly what has been suggested, but they will respond somehow. As you give yourself some of the suggestions from this book, you may not always respond immediately to the exact suggestion. You can feel confident, however, that you will respond eventually in your own way: mediately.

Throughout the chapters of this book you will experiment with many forms of suggestion. Some may find that they respond best to direct approaches, others may prefer subtle, indirect methods. Experiment. Contemplate what happens. What works best for you? Try to notice subtle, mediate effects as well as the more obvious immediate ones. Accept what your individuality gives you. Hypnotic learning takes place in the mind of the subject. Associations to a suggested idea can be helpful, not just your immediate response to the suggestion. Observe and note your own reactions and tendencies. With time you will be able to predict your responses better.

Indirect Suggestion

Erickson and Rossi delineated many of the parameters of indirect suggestion in a number of volumes, (1976, 1979, 1980) to mobilize and activate latent potential from the unconscious, bypassing consciousness.

Coué used the conscious mind to activate unconscious potentials through the imagination. The Nancy School emphasized automatic ideomotor response to bring about changes. Braid utilized focusing of attention to enhance suggestive responsiveness. Erickson creatively enlisted these and many other natural mechanisms of the mind, trusting that unconsciously, patients would find their own best ways to free themselves from problematic difficulties and discover new, creative ways of coping. Erickson appreciated individuality.

Unconscious functioning can be intelligent, creative, healthy, and free (Erickson, Rossi, 1980). Education in unconscious functioning involves learning to permit responses to indirect suggestion. People can outgrow problems by utilizing their own repertoire of learnings and capacities which they may not even know they have. Unhampered by learned limitations, trance returns individuals to their unconscious as a foundation from which new potentials in behaviors, thoughts, and attitudes are created.

There are many forms of indirect suggestion: open-ended suggestions, compound and contingent suggestions, acceptance set, and binds, to name a few. Some of them can be creatively adapted to self hypnosis. Simple exercises in each form follow, but more complex applications must wait until you have tried trance, since indirect suggestion involves unconscious processing.

In general, indirect forms of suggestion utilize the subject's tendency to mediate or actually construct his own hypnotic responses out of the stimuli and suggestions preferred by the operator. (Erickson, Rossi 1980, 454)

This concept can be applied in self hypnosis as you develop an open attitude towards your inner self. Using indirect suggestion in self hypnosis requires that you set the stage for yourself with the general concept of suggestion. You can create both the specific description of the suggestion and the expected response, outside of awareness, intuitively.

Open-Ended Suggestions

Open-ended suggestions work well for self hypnosis along with trance. Conscious direct self suggestion without trance can also use them, but not as effectively. When unconscious processes are dominant during trance, open-ended suggestions are guided by the unconscious, inner needs. The indirect approach teaches you to appreciate that by trusting your unconscious to be helpful, a therapeutic process can gather momentum. As your personality becomes more positive, self actualization tends to guide therapy.

The self actualization process is similar to Gestalt Therapy's organismic self-regulating mechanism. There are inner signals to pay attention and do something about. Attending to these inner signals gradually leads to homeostasis, the natural balancing tendency towards health and maturity. By resolving important concerns, people are freed to make their lives more satisfying. Inner signals guide this process: tensions, discomforts, as well as comfortable feelings. The meaning of inner signals is not always clear, but they point the way to health and maturation intuitively.

Open-Ended Suggestion

Offer a suggestion with many possible responses. For example, "I wonder whether I could have an experience in my hand. It could become light, heavy, warm, cool. I don't know what I will feel, but will wait for my response."

Compound and Contingent Suggestions

In their simplest form, compound suggestions are made up of two statements connected by "and". (Erickson, Rossi, Rossi, 1976)

Contingent/Compound Suggestion

Contingent suggestions involve two usually unrelated suggestions which you relate together, one dependent on the other, for hypnotic experience. Experiment with the example to hold your arm out and suggest to yourself, "As I hold my arm out it becomes heavier and heavier." In this example a contingent link between holding out the arm and a suggested effect is made.

Binds

Bind suggestions are numerous and potentially complex in their nature. For self hypnosis some binds can be used, but others are difficult to perform on yourself. The following bind exercise can be helpful in learning to apply binds in self hypnosis.

Bind Exercise

Sit comfortably and place your hands on your knees. Pay careful attention to your right hand, then your left hand, and ask which one will be lighter, which heavier. Wait for your response; wonder which one will do what. You cannot anticipate. Each time is a new time.

Posthypnotic Suggestion

Suggestion can also be applied posthypnotically, which means it is to take effect after the trance is terminated. Posthypnotic suggestion is a field of application that derives naturally from trance work, allowing unconscious factors to take effect. Erickson and Erickson (1941) in an interesting study of this phenomenon, noted that posthypnotic suggestion tends to induce a trance when it takes effect. Their definition is most useful:

> *A posthypnotic act has been found to be one performed by the hypnotic subject after awakening from a trance, in response to suggestions given during the trance state, with the execution of the act marked by an absence of any demonstrable conscious awareness in the subject of the underlying cause and motive for his act. (Erickson and Rossi 1980, 388)*

The posthypnotic act may spontaneously induce a brief trance, linked to the performance of the act. After a posthypnotic response, trance can be easily evoked. Posthypnotic behavior can be used in self hypnosis to enhance your trance learnings. Various factors may affect this phenomenon. Experiment to discover the most effective ways for you to respond. Start with a simple posthypnotic suggestion that permits time and individualization of response, using open-ended suggestions. Try applying varieties of posthypnotic suggestions. As response to one posthypnotic suggestion is gained, try several suggestions in succession.

Posthypnotic Suggestions

Suggest that next time you try self hypnosis it will be easier for you to go into trance. You can also suggest that following trance you will feel more relaxed and calm. Try other positive and useful suggestions, as your ability to respond evolves.

Enhancing the Success of Suggestions

An important factor affecting whether a suggestion is accepted or rejected involves the mental set of the person at the time of the suggestion. Positive thinking, a school of practical, applied philosophy in the late 1800's and early 1900's conceptualized that the positive or negative atmosphere created by thoughts about the world create a characteristic set leading to a tendency for personal destiny to evolve in a positive or negative way. Positive thinking contained a core of useful understandings about life. If people expect the worst to happen, they may unintentionally tend to bring it about through unconscious ideomotor mechanisms, paradoxically confirming their belief. Therapy entails altering expectations in a positive direction so that people develop hopeful and positive expectations towards the future. (Frank, 1973) Then the ideomotor mechanism works in their favor.

Negative expectancies lead peoples' imagination away from the positive potential in their situations. Instead, they may feel discouraged from tackling challenges wholeheartedly with the limited resources they perceive in themselves. Suggestion aims at these expectancies, to turn them around. Positive expectations encourage transcendence of mediocre functioning, to open the door to unrealized potentials. With a positive attitude, adverse circumstances transform into challenging invitations to outgrow narrow boundaries of adjustment. Positive thinking is useful.

Suggestion in Context

Suggestion takes effect within the total context, the suggestion situation. The boundaries are the person giving the suggestion, the person receiving the suggestion, and the circumstances at the time (Weitzenhoffer, 1957).

Many factors affect how we respond to suggestions. Suggestibility is mostly a function of the individual perceptual field, influenced by the setting or circumstances. We understand simple, clear circumstances and therefore can react to simple problems with our rational faculties. But increases in ambiguity and complexity may lead to failure to understand things consciously. Openness in the surroundings is one of the important factors in response to suggestion. If our situation or circumstance is filled with unknown or has a great deal of ambiguity in meaning, we cannot respond rationally. Complexity and ambiguity lead us scan for parameters to help interpret matters. We grope for cues. In this state of indecision and frustration there is a tendency to be especially sensitive to suggestion. Consequently, complex problems may require suggestive assistance, which can incorporate the greater wisdom of unconscious processes.

Suggestibility and Hypnotic Susceptibility

A time-honored dispute in psychology is that between nature and nurture. This applies to susceptibility and suggestibility. Some believe that susceptibility and suggestibility are determined by genetic factors, that a person is born a suggestible type. Others hold that nurture is more primary, that people can learn to become more responsive to suggestion and hypnosis through practice and experience. Still others hold that it is a combination of the two, with an individual balance between them. We have found that each person has natural ability expressed in individual talents. Each individual's natural abilities can be used as starting points for new learnings and possibilities. Further evolution is always possible. Unconscious potential is limitless.

There are many differences in experimental findings concerning suggestibility and hypnotizability. Research has not always confirmed with certainty definitive traits of suggestibility or hypnotizability, though hypnotizability tends to remain constant (Weitzenhoffer, 1953). Certain factors are generally accepted as indicative of high hypnotizability. The Stanford Hypnotic Susceptibility Scales of Hilgard have been widely accepted. High scorers are characterized as capable of being highly imaginative, often creative, involved, adventuresome, and spontaneous, healthy personality traits (Josephine Hilgard, 1970). Diamond (1974) holds that hypnotizability is not a constant, but rather appears to be a learnable skill that can be enhanced. In exploratory self hypnosis or clinical hypnosis, scales of susceptibility can be used to help as maps and guides in locating talents and deficits in hypnotic functioning, rather than to set limits that become the parameters of abilities.

Erickson preferred a simple and clear indicator: response attentiveness. In self hypnosis, the task and at times, the challenge, is to develop your capacities further, through careful, sensitive, creative exploration.

Erickson explained in an early paper:

Personal experience extending over 35 years with well over 3500 hypnotic subjects has been most convincing of the importance of subject individuality and time values.

One of the author's most capable subjects required less than 30 seconds to develop his first profound trance, with subsequent equally rapid and consistently reliable hypnotic behavior. A second remarkably competent subject required 300 hours of systematic labor before a trance was even induced; thereafter, a 20-30 minute period of trance induction was requisite to secure. valid hypnotic behavior. (Erickson in Haley 1967)

⌘

Creative artistry in communication and technique, coupled with sincere rapport with your inner nature and needs, leads to good response to self suggestion. No factor or condition restricts your response to self hypnosis. If the willingness and motivation to experiment are present, you can develop an ability to respond, unless there is a hidden inward reason not to. If you cannot respond, or you feel blocked and uncomfortable, you should not attempt to force matters. Ideomotor questioning may help you discover answers when carefully and sensitively applied. Sometimes, professional support may be necessary to help in problem solving and therapeutic changes. At other times, self support and continued development through self hypnosis may be adequate. Use appropriate resources with unconscious intelligence.

PART THREE

Pathways to Trance

The mind is a reservoir of positive potential with unexplored, new capacities as well as lost and forgotten abilities from earlier years. Receptivity to potential from the unconscious requires a different pathway than conscious knowing. This can be learned, just as one learns to differentiate feelings, meanings, colors or any other sense data. Use this method of self hypnosis to show you how to recognize your capacities, both conscious and unconscious, and find your pathway to trance.

Six

Steps to Self Hypnosis
Rapport with Your
Unconscious Mind in Trance

Consciousness can never be certain of what is going to be experienced, but it can learn to interact constructively with whatever altered mode of functioning the unconscious makes available. (Erickson & Rossi, Vol. I 1980, 132)

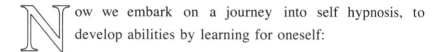ow we embark on a journey into self hypnosis, to develop abilities by learning for oneself:

Where the learner experiences fascination with some aspect of the world, envisioned in the mode of possibility...Independent learning is the embodiment and implementation of imaginative fascination...he experiences himself as beckoned, challenged, invited, fascinated by the possibility. (Jourard 1968, 112)

Through the exercises in this chapter you can enhance and develop your talents for self hypnosis, helping to create possibilities for trance. Everyone has individual talents: some are good dancers, others can draw accurately, while others are good at calculations. Similarly, we also have unconscious talents we may know nothing about. We take these abilities for granted, as we just express them. Some people are naturally able to relax, some can easily develop visual hallucinations such as seeing colors when they close their eyes, while others can forget or remember readily. Unconscious tendencies are not always recognized as potential talents and may even be considered problems or shortcomings. Forgetfulness might seem to be a difficulty, but sometimes forgetting clears the way to remember what is important. Properly applied and worked with hypnotically, unconscious tendencies can be useful talents that lead to change and growth.

Approach these exercises with an open mind. You may find some exercises seem easier than others. Consider your efforts to be like an exploratory scientific experiment. You begin with the gathering of data to he analyzed at a later time. Observe and notice thoughts, experiences, and reactions. These will become individual building blocks for trance. Do not pass judgment or draw conclusions while still collecting data. Allow time for them to be viewed as meaningful parts of a whole.

Do one exercise at a time, followed by reading of commentary. If you prefer, read ahead, then return to the exercises. Do not overload, as there is no advantage in hurrying through. Cultivate sensitivity to your personal rhythms and timing.

Read the entire exercise several times, then set the book aside. Make yourself comfortable and try what you remember from the exercise. Do not be concerned with what you forget. Encourage your unconscious to have positive experiences with the exercises.

Preliminary Exercises

Theoretical understanding of the unconscious is only one aspect of the learnings necessary for mastery of self hypnosis. Experiencing is even more primary, for the unconscious is sensed experientially.

Giving yourself a few minutes to settle before every exercise is helpful, especially before your first exercise. People do not usually notice how tense they are during the day unless someone gives them feedback. Instead, they adapt and continue on. These first exercises attempt to bring you in touch with your level of tension and teach you to let go as you feel able.

Preparation for Trance

Sit or lie down and relax for a few moments. As you relax, let your thoughts drift and your attention roam wherever it likes. Try not to get lost in any one thought-path; simply notice associations and let them go. Do this until you notice some settling or calming.

Exercise in Everyday Out of Awareness Unconscious

To explore the unconscious as it manifests itself in everyday life, turn your attention to your hands. You probably were not thinking about your hands, but now that we mention them, you become aware of whatever sensations you are having. Perhaps your hands feel cold, or tingly or maybe light. You cannot accurately guess what you will experience without simply paying attention and waiting for the response. The experience occurs in its own way and in its own time. Sometimes it is interesting to place one hand on each knee and pay attention to the weight of each hand. You might find that one hand feels immediately lighter or heavier than the other, or that at first they seem the same, but as you pay attention one becomes heavier than the other. You may be surprised by your unconscious response. While you are waiting for one hand to become lighter you might discover unexpectedly that one hand becomes cooler, or maybe you have a new experience of your hand feeling very far away, or growing larger. You will respond in your own unique way. Your conscious mind does not know how this will be. As you learn to allow and be attentive to your spontaneous responses you will become acquainted with your natural unconscious which you can then learn to develop.

Exercise in Peripheral Associations

Relax once again. This time try to recall how you felt after you completed the previous exercise. Picture yourself sitting or lying comfortably and remember how your hands felt. Wait until you feel ready to try the exercise. As you focus on this, you will probably find your body beginning to relax a little. While thinking about the previous experience peripheral thoughts probably flicker in the back of your mind. Shift attention to a peripheral thought or experience. For example, as dinner-hour approaches, notice if a vague thought or image is present about food. Perhaps you realize you are thinking about a pleasant moment. These less obvious thoughts are present peripherally, but you usually do not bring them into consciousness. In this exercise, try to mentally reach for those flickering thoughts as they appear briefly in the stream of awareness.

To work with this, let your thoughts drift for a moment. If you notice a flicker into awareness that you cannot quite recognize, invite yourself to have a feeling, an image, or a thought, a clue. As you become more at ease with your unconscious you will be surprised to discover that your unconscious will supply you with a relevant thought or image even if the direct connection is not obvious.

For example, a client came for hypnotherapy to help her cope with a stressful, uncomfortable adaptation to her marriage, job and family. During therapeutic trance we suggested that she have a meaningful image, something that could help her understand and outgrow her problems. First she saw lights, mostly white streaks. Then she felt an intense nauseous feeling. After she awoke from trance, she described this with dismay. She thought that she had not been able to produce an image, as requested. She worried that she was incapable of imagery. She did not realize that her unconscious actually was very responsive, expressing meaning in a way personally meaningful to her, using vague rather than obvious symbolic analogy. Later she discovered her feeling of nausea had a hidden significance.

Discovering Your Perceptual Mode

People tend to perceive in one perceptual mode more than another. For example, someone might characteristically say, "That feels right," or "I want to get in touch with that." This person tends to orient kinesthetically, that is, by feelings and sensations. Another person might say, "I see your point. That looks good." This is a visual orientation. A third type will use metaphors like, "Did you hear about this?" or "I hear that." They usually can clearly recall the sound of someone's voice. They tend to orient auditorily, using imaginative hearing. These are the three main perceptual systems of orientation. Taste and smell can be used to orient, although somewhat less. Combinations and individual variations are also possible.

Some people do not orient perceptually, but tend to orient conceptually. Experiences are filtered through concepts without noticing perceptions directly. These kinds of people will say, " I think this is a beautiful day." Their thoughts about their perceptions are most central.

We use all of these modes at various times, but typically process more with one mode than another. The exercise that follows will familiarize you with your own spontaneous mode of choice used for perceiving and processing.

Perceptual Mode Exercise

Sit quietly and relax, as in the other exercises. Now recall the moment when you first opened this book. Think about it for a moment, remembering as much about it as you can. Notice how you recall: Do you see a picture of the pages or your hands opening the cover? Do you remember how you were feeling, maybe tired, sore, wide awake, happy, or curious about the content. Perhaps you remembered the sound of the pages as you turned them or the song that was playing on the radio or the noise from the street outside. Or you may recall what you were thinking, such as the plans for the day or your ideas about hypnosis. If you saw a picture, you probably tend to orient visually. If you felt sensation, you may be more kinesthetic. If you heard sounds, you tend to orient through the auditory mode. If you experienced a series of thoughts, you are probably more conceptual. You may have combinations of these as well. Try this experiment a few times during the day using different memories and different tasks to double-check your results. Look for consistent patterns.

Once you determine your favorite mode, use this in the early exercises when there is a choice given. Later, you are encouraged to develop other modes. Each mode offers a richness in experience and alternative inroads into the unconscious. You may be surprised to discover that you have been limiting yourself to only one. Other modes of experience can also become comfortable and natural. We use our usual mode as our map, for orienting in new territory. After you become familiar with your unconscious you will not need to be restricted to this one mode.

Body Image Alterations

People take their body image for granted as a fixed reality. Unless we have a change in our usual body experience our general sensation of body image often goes unnoticed. Chapter 4 described this in relation to the unconscious. Hypnosis can allow you to experience and work with changes in body image, to creatively apply these learnings to related problems.

Preparation for Body Image Alteration

Sit or lie down quietly. Let all of your muscles settle. Recall whether you had a stronger auditory (hearing), visual (seeing), kinesthetic (feeling), or conceptual (thinking) response in the previous exercise. You can use your preferred mode to achieve maximal relaxation for you. Your unconscious will regulate the level. Try not to prevent your natural response from occurring. Honest curiosity about what this experience will be like, helps. Wonder how you will feel. Wait for your response.

Trance: Self Hypnosis Exercise Series

You have done a number of preliminary exercises that developed some component skills for the hypnotic experience. Now you are ready to begin learning self hypnosis.

Find a quiet and comfortable place where you can do this without pressure or interruption for at least fifteen minutes. Knowing that you will be trying your first trance, you may feel excited or nervous. Glance inwardly now to note any attitudes you might have about doing self hypnosis. Or you might wish to pay attention to your feelings about trance, or perhaps listen to the inner dialogue of your thoughts: What are your reactions? Sometimes people have superstitions about the powers of hypnosis from television and movies, about how it can take control of the mind. Research indicates that no one has ever been harmed by hypnosis itself (Kroger 1977, 104). Hypnosis allows you to be in touch with inner needs and motivations. You will not do or experience anything that is inconsistent with your true nature, including your ethics and morals. It is reassuring to realize that personality remains constant. You do not change your nature, just to be hypnotized.

At first, you can help yourself awaken from trance by counting backwards from five to one. With each number, as you approach one, you will become more alert, all your sensations returning to normal. If you finish but continue to feel unusual sensations, wait for a few minutes. Then if you need to, close your eyes again and go back into trance for a minute or two. Suggest that your sensations will now return to normal and again count backwards from five to one. Transitions in and out of trance become smoother and easier with practice.

As you grow more familiar with hypnosis you may not need to count your way out of trance. We may not explicitly tell you to count backwards after each exercise that follows, but use this technique if it helps make the transition to being awake easier. You may evolve your own way.

Getting Set

Imagine for a moment what you expect trance to feel like. People sometimes say that they expect to relax, to feel calm, to have their body become cool or warm, to become light or tingly. If you discovered in the earlier exercises that you tend to orient visually, try a visual image. Picture yourself in trance. Would you look relaxed? Are your eyes open or closed? Use your perceptual mode to imagine yourself in trance.

Notice your response. Does it surprise you or is it consistent with your expectations? If you truly feel surprised, you have probably had a genuine unconscious response.

Now, using your mode of choice, experiment with going into trance.

Listening to Trance

Recall a sound of nature, like the ocean waves, a bubbling brook, the quiet of a winter's snow fall, the wind rustling through the trees, or any other sound which you have enjoyed. Focus your attention on this but do not hurry the sound. Simply wait for it to fill out, to become even fuller or perhaps to alter in some way you do not expect. While you listen, your body can relax even more deeply. Your muscles settle, letting go of any unnecessary tension. Continue listening, allowing any other images, thoughts, or feelings to develop as well. Deepen the experience when you feel ready. Continue to relax deeply. Let your thoughts drift. When you feel ready, bring yourself out of trance until you feel fully alert.

Seeing Trance

Recall an image or a place you have been and really enjoyed. Perhaps a vacation spot, a hideaway in the mountains, a secluded beach, a forest. Picture the beauty; look at the colors; walk around and reacquaint yourself with it. You would be relaxed if you went there, so your body can relax while you picture this place. You might see these images vividly or they could be vague wisps of pictures and colors flickering past. However they appear, you can enhance the experience with a very comfortable feeling of relaxation all over. Picture yourself relaxing even more as you wonder how deeply relaxed you can become. Let your thoughts drift. When you feel ready, bring yourself out of trance until you feel fully alert.

Feeling Trance

You will probably find your attention wandering to the feeling in your body, and recall a very nice feeling of calm, both inner and outer. Ask all of your muscles to settle and relax. Can you silently recall a time in your life when you felt totally at ease, calm, and comfortable? Perhaps a clear memory will come to mind or only a vague recollection. Recall where you were, as in the previous mode exercises, but focus on the feeling you had in your body, of calmness or happiness. Fill out the details naturally with memories of the sensations, or other relevant feelings. You may be curious and interested in just what it would be like to relax deeper than you ever have before. Wait for the response as you continue to imagine that calm, comfortable feeling. Let your thoughts drift. When you feel ready, bring yourself out of trance until you feel fully alert.

In the exercises that follow we may ask you to imagine an image. You might respond with a feeling, thought, a sound, or perhaps nothing at all. Keep in mind that these are all legitimate responses--your inroads into a working relationship with your unconscious. These links between conscious and unconscious are the keys to successfully learning and applying self hypnosis.

If you have had difficulty thus far with the exercises, shift to Chapter 7 on resistance, then return here after you have experimented with defenses and resistance.

Trance Ratification

The trance experience is not always easy to recognize at first. You may have noticed that you were relaxed and calm but may feel that this is not anything unusual or different from ordinary waking. Confirmation that trance is happening helps to intensify the experience and leads to an increase in trance abilities. Erickson and Rossi refer to this as trance ratification. (Chapter 2) Ideomotor signaling is useful for this.

Exercise in Ideomotor Signaling

Sit or lie down so that your hands rest either on your legs or by your side. Experiment with one of the previous exercises where you felt responsive. Invite yourself to become even more relaxed than before. Once you feel comfortable, focus on your hands. Consider how frequently people move their hands in conversation without thinking about it. Sometimes the gesture is even more meaningful than the words. Do you talk with your hands? Now, ask your unconscious a "yes" or "no" question. Designate one hand as "yes" and the other hand as "no." Choose a question for which you do not have the answer, such as: Would my unconscious like my legs to relax? Could I feel tingling in my fingertips? Can I have a pleasant memory? Could I see colors when I close my eyes? Now, wait and pay close attention to your hands. Do not try to move them, simply notice. Sometimes people feel the answer as tingling, lightness, or heaviness in one hand or the other. Sometimes a person will notice warmth or coolness. Still others will feel a finger raise in one hand or the other or maybe a feeling jumps from one hand to the other and back again. After a little while you will know what your response has been, and in which hand. If you felt something in your hand, you unconsciously answered the question.

This exercise may not be what you expected or exactly as you predicted. These mysteries make communicating with your unconscious interesting. Your conscious does not know what your unconscious already knows. In his seminars, Erickson often said, "Your unconscious mind knows a lot more than you."

Hand Levitation

Lightness and movement developing in a finger, hand, or arm are components of a classic hypnotic phenomenon called hand levitation. The finger, hand, or arm feels as if it is moving by itself. You do not need to do anything in particular except to allow it to occur naturally. People who tend to use the kinesthetic mode may find this easier to do, but anyone can learn to experience it with practice. Hand levitation is done by following each successful action in sequence, gathering momentum. All that you have already learned will help to channel and shape your response. These exercises can be repeated as often as you like, at different sessions.

Exercise in Hand Levitation

Sit or lie down in such a way that your hands and arms are comfortable and free to move. If you are sitting, let a hand rest palm down on each kneecap. If you are lying down, place your hands down by your side or folded across your body. Do not restrain one hand with the other. Loosen your muscles, and focus attention on your hands. Notice any experiencing you begin to have in your hands. One common feeling is a tingling in the fingertips. You might compare your two hands: Does one hand feel more tingly, or perhaps lighter, heavier, warmer, or cooler? Stay with the experience and ask your unconscious what it would be like for the tingling, warming, or whatever you feel, to begin to lead to a feeling of lightness. You may feel as if something is tugging on your finger, thumb, or hand, like a helium balloon tied to your finger or wrist. You may begin to feel a very nice lightness that gets lighter and lighter with every breath. Perhaps the tingling increases, bringing about movement. Do not inhibit the movement. Follow this experience sensitively, and let your fingers begin to raise. Stay with it and invite the lightness to increase and your hand to raise even higher. If you like, suggest that your hand lifts all the way up to touch your face. When it does, your relaxation in trance deepens more than before.

Give yourself time to allow these sensations to develop. You do not know which hand will respond and just what it will be like, but you can, as in previous exercises, become increasingly curious as to how your unconscious will respond. Many creative variations are possible.

A client underwent hypnosis to learn to control his temper. He was an intelligent lawyer whose temper was interfering with his professional and personal life. Before the trance, we discussed hand levitation as one hypnotic phenomenon he could learn from. He said he was curious about it but thought it would be very difficult to actually do. He developed a comfortable trance and even smiled as he entered trance. Hand levitation was suggested in a similar manner to how it is described above. His hands barely moved, if at all, but his face became flushed and a few beads of sweat appeared on his brow. Upon awakening he recounted what he referred to as a "marvelous experience." He said that the levitation was so powerful that he was doing jumping jacks! The experience was vivid for him. He felt as if he had exerted tremendous energy. He was extremely pleased to realize that he could have such an intense experience in his imagination. This was pivotal in the moderation of his temper. This taught him that he could think an angry thought but not have to express it in action. He learned that control was possible for him.

Hypnotic phenomena do not always correlate with what they seem to be. An experience can become a metaphor, a symbol, or lead to something new, an inspiration for growth and learning.

Visual Imagery and Hallucination

Visual images in trance are natural phenomena of hypnosis. Most people can learn to see visual imagery, even though it might be easier for some than for others. Vividness in mental imagery is a natural talent, but can be developed further with correct practice.

A classic method for entering trance is by using something to look at. The hypnotic subject is encouraged to look at an object that can fascinate, like a crystal, a lit candle, or a turning spiral. Use whatever interests you. We have often used abstract paintings such as the ones in this book. Milton Erickson used a beautiful quartz crystal on his desk for patients to look at. Be imaginative.

Exercise in Hallucination

To begin, look at the object carefully. Study it, noticing all its components, the colors, the shapes. Next look at the outline, then the interior. Watch very carefully, focusing all your attention on the object. As you concentrate fully on it, your thoughts can drift. Think about the object, look at the object, study it. As you watch, you can let your body relax, your breathing rate settle. Let your eyes move around the object after you have studied all the different components. Can you see any alterations in the object as you watch? For example, you may see blurring, a change in the colors, or an alteration in shape. Perhaps you notice aspects you did not see before. How does the object appear to alter? Try suggesting a change that you would be curious to experience and wait for your response. Then relax your vision and let yourself return to normal seeing.

Interesting objects are often looked at as an hypnotic technique. However, since hypnosis is an inner experience, seek the image within.

Exercise in Inner Imagery

In this exercise, begin by relaxing your body as before. You might like to try this exercise following the previous one. As you are looking at your chosen object, imagine your eyelids becoming heavy. Suggest that your eyelids grow heavier and heavier. Wait for your eyes to feel ready to close. Then allow your eyelids to close. If they don't want to after a long wait, close your eyes anyway. Relax your eyelids and allow your entire body to relax very deeply.

It is possible to visualize color in formless, abstract, or symbolic form. At first the color may appear as just one shade. Gradually it could alter in its shade, depth, or even change colors. Sometimes people see a kaleidoscope of color. Other times it is simply white or black afterimages, lights, or streaks. Experiment with offering a suggestion for a color you would like to experience. Wait for your response. Watch it evolve.

Anesthesia & Hyperaesthesia

Anesthesia is a well documented hypnotic phenomenon. It has been used in medicine by qualified practitioners for surgery as the sole anesthetic. For example, there is an educational film from the 1950's showing a woman undergoing her fourth Cesarean birth under hypnosis with no pain. Hypnosis was used predominantly in surgery before the discovery of chloroform, as pointed out in Chapter 1.

Classically anesthesia has been produced by direct suggestion, relying upon the subject's suggestibility. Hypnotic effectiveness does not only depend upon suggestibility. Other factors play an important part.

Motivation can enhance the ability to produce anesthesia. A client who was working on an intense personality change used hypnosis occasionally to relax. She did not think she was very good at hypnosis and even doubted its efficacy. She was an intelligent woman in her late twenties who suffered from intense anxiety. She felt stuck in an uncomfortable job and living situation. She tended to be judgmental, especially toward herself. During the course of treatment she had to get a tooth extracted.

She decided to give hypnosis a try without the use of narcotics. She had no idea before the appointment how she would cope with only local anesthesia. She reported at her session following the dental work that she felt nervous at first, but that once in the chair she went into trance. She spontaneously imagined little creatures in her mouth with brooms, rolling big balls of pain away. While she viewed this amusing image, she became calm. She handled the procedure well and needed no narcotics or pain killers afterwards. She had not expected to use an image, especially such a seemingly silly one, but it worked. Even her dentist laughed when she told him. Pain is a sensation that hypnosis can affect in many complex ways. Prepare well before you attempt to apply these skills in practice. Do not substitute for good professional care. Make it better.

Exercise to Practice Anesthesia
with Direct Suggestion

Find a comfortable level of trance, suggesting relaxation and comfort of the body. Decide where you would like to produce the anesthesia: a hand? head? foot? etc. Next you can give yourself a suggestion in a mode which you have used successfully before, or you might want to experiment with something new. You could recall a time when you were out in very cold temperatures, and after a period of time your nose and cheeks became so cold that they were numb. Recall the tingling followed by a nothing feeling. Suggest that the body part is tingling as it becomes colder and colder until you can no longer feel it.

Sometimes you can produce anesthesia by dissociating from that body part. Imagine that your hand, arm, or wherever you have chosen, is feeling far away from the rest of your body. You might feel as if the hand is growing in size at first, then seems to take on an unreal or distant quality. Some subjects improve watching themselves from a distance. One client felt like he left his body sitting in the session and went to the beach. Some people feel tingly or temperature alterations before the hand or arm begins to feel distant or numb. You can test yourself once you feel that you have achieved an adequate anesthesia by touching the anesthetized body part.

Hyperaesthesia

Many know hypnosis can reduce sensations, but few realize that hypnosis can also enhance sensations. This can be very useful in some circumstances. A young man in his twenties, teeming with excess energy, came for hypnotherapy. He had lost his job and decided to start his own business working with machinery. He spoke quickly, moved around during the sessions, and described himself as "hyper." In his new business, he complained that sometimes he would miss a small detail which caused him to have to return to the job site to redo the work. All profit was lost, and at times it even cost him money to complete the job. He was inattentive to the important details of his work, yet over attentive to unimportant details. He needed to improve.

He learned to go into trance and found himself enjoying the calm and relaxation he felt. During trance we suggested that he imagine a place where he felt very comfortable. He thought of the woods near where he grew up. He recalled every detail: the woods noises, the smell of the leaves and plants, the colors of the sun shining through the trees. He searched back in his memory to carefully recall many details, focusing all his energy on sensitizing himself to the experience. The week after this trance he reported he was surprised to discover something new. Seemingly automatically, he found himself listening intently, looking carefully, and noticing exact details in the machinery he was fixing. He reported he could hear minute sounds indicating where the malfunction occurred. His exacting attentiveness resulted in a week with no callbacks, no errors. We asked him to focus on his body, feel his shin, notice how long his arms were, his legs, to feel his breathing. This evolved his learnings further. He learned to become so sensitive that he could feel a whisper of a breeze or a minute touch to his arm. He gained greater skill with tools. Hyperaesthesia can be developed in trance, to apply in useful ways in your life.

Exercise in Hyperaesthesia

Begin with a memory, perhaps a place or an experience you enjoyed or one that happened very recently. Now consider what it would be like to recall details of the experience which you had forgotten. Concentrate on sense memories such as taste, smell, touch, or sound. Was there a bird or cricket chirping? Did the waves pound at the ocean? Can you recall the sound of a friend's voice? Wait for a memory to appear. Request that it become even clearer.

Time Distortion

Another natural ability of the unconscious is time distortion. Everyone has felt the minutes slowly ticking, waited in line, sat through a dull class, or endured a boring dinner party.

Conversely, there are times when the hours pass too quickly, and we wonder what happened to the day. These are both examples of the mind's natural ability to alter the experience of time.

If the average person were asked to define time, he or she would probably think of time as it seems on a clock. However, suppose a class of students were asked how long the duration of a class session seemed. The answers would vary greatly. The interested, involved student would probably report a shorter seeming duration than the bored disinterested student. Time distortion occurs when the seeming duration of a time interval is different from the clock time of that interval. Time distortion can appear to be either shorter or longer, depending upon the experience. Both are natural and can be utilized for creative and therapeutic applications.

Milton Erickson and Linn Cooper (Cooper & Erickson 1982, 20-22) did extensive research on this phenomenon. They carefully set up experimental definitions of time distortion to refer to the discrepancy between clock time and experiential time over a given time interval. During one experiment a trance subject was instructed to go to a cotton field and pick four rows of cotton, counting the bolls as she picked them, one at a time. The subject was not to hurry. She was instructed to raise her hand when she finished. She raised her hand 217 seconds after starting and reported 719 cotton bolls. She stated that she seemed to have been working for one hour and twenty minutes.

The second experiment involved the same task, except the experimenter put a time limit on the task. The time allotted was three seconds. The subject reported that she had picked 862 bolls and that it seemed like an entire hour and twenty minutes. In both experiments, the subject had a time distortion experience.

The following exercises will illustrate both the experience of time going faster and that of time slowing down. Each has its application and use. For example, speeding up the experience of time can be very useful for pain control, slowing it down can make it possible to accomplish more efficiently.

Preliminary Exercise in Time Distortion

Go into trance, relax, and be comfortable. Think about time for a moment. Picture the hands of a clock. Watch them move for a five-minute period. Wonder whether you could tell the difference between thirty-two minutes and thirty-three minutes, or if you could distinguish an interval of five seconds from six. Think about a time when you were very bored and time seemed to move very slowly. You may have felt this while waiting for something to happen. Now recall a time when the hours passed so quickly that looking back, the event seemed over before it started. Holidays often leave people with this experience. Let your mind drift and associations flow freely. Relax very deeply. When you are ready, clear your mind of thought for a moment. Perhaps you would like to imagine a lake settling, where all the mud sinks to the bottom. The water becomes crystal clear, like your mind can be. When you are ready, wake up refreshed and alert.

Exercise in Slowing down Time

You can give yourself a basic experience in time distortion. Find a quiet place outdoors where you can walk comfortably and alone (or without speaking if you are with someone) for what feels like fifteen minutes. Do not try to direct your attention anywhere in particular. When it seems fifteen minutes have passed, stop and check your watch. Immediately following, take a walk in a busy place where you are comfortable doing this, for what feels like fifteen minutes. Again, let your attention float, unfocused. Do not look at your watch until you think you have walked for at least fifteen minutes. Afterwards, note what you experienced, and return home. If you had a difference between experienced time and clock time, you have felt time distortion.

Imaginative Time Distortion

Next available session time find a comfortable place to sit and relax. Allow yourself to go comfortably into trance. Once you feel that you have found inner calm, recall your two walks. Think back on the surroundings of each, one at a time, and try to visualize yourself there again. Some people will actually feel as if they are re-enacting the walk. Assure yourself that you have all the time you need to take the walks, and do not rush. Follow this procedure for each of the two walks. When you have completed one, wake up, noting how long the walk seemed to take. Check the time on the clock and compare with your experienced time. Next imagine the second walk. Again check the time on the clock and compare.

Trance Time Distortion

Check the clock before you go into trance. Let an image occur to you, any image or scene. While you watch, other images may appear, one after another. Let these images become as vivid as they can until you feel as if you are right there in the scene. Follow the scene until you feel ready to clear your mind of all images. You might suggest a blank, a black nothingness, or a bright light. Play with the possibilities as you wait for your response and enjoy deep relaxation. When you are ready, awaken relaxed and refreshed. Note how much time you felt passed, then compare to the actual time it took. Repeat this exercise a few times at different sessions, attempting to make the images more and more vivid.

Trance Time Distortion II

Go into trance and visualize yourself doing an activity which normally takes a fixed amount of clock time to complete. You can choose from one of the following three examples, or choose one of your own: 1) Swim laps, jog, ride a bike, etc. for fifteen to twenty minutes. 2) Cook breakfast including all preparations for fifteen to twenty minutes. (Let someone else do the dishes) 3) Watch the first quarter of a football game or any other favorite sport. Another possibility is to watch the first act of a play you enjoy.

You have practiced this kind of trance phenomenon several times. Make your choice as to what you will imagine doing. If you prefer another activity that takes about fifteen to twenty minutes, use it. When you have found a comfortable level of trance, begin the imaginative activity. Allow yourself to become intensely interested in performing it. Take your time and work to the best of your ability. Do not hurry. Try to be thorough.

Remember to note the time before you go into trance and when you awaken. When you have finished, clear your mind. Wake up refreshed and alert. You can repeat this exercise a few times at various sittings. Try to use what feels like fifteen to twenty minutes. If you notice a discrepancy between clock time and experienced time, you have felt time distortion.

Frequently people will experience time expansion with these exercises. However, both time expansion and time constriction are useful tools. One of our clients had an experience with time distortion that clarifies its surprising benefits. She wanted to lose weight. She was working for a large company while she was going to school in the evenings to become a health care worker. She told us she disliked her job and felt like the time dragged by each day. She felt she barely had any time for herself or her school work. Some coworkers who were also consulting us for hypnosis at the same time, reported they experienced her as hard to get along with at work.

Throughout treatment she went into a very deep trance and always had total amnesia for her trance experience. We taught her time distortion similar to the exercises in this chapter. Her unconscious spontaneously came up with a creative solution to her dilemma. At her next session she reported a surprising discovery. She found that work had changed. The day seemed to speed by. But strangely, after she got home in the evening she felt she had all the time she could need. Weekends went by slowly and leisurely, filled with extra time. As the weeks passed she found, much to her surprise, work grew to be more and more pleasant for her because it went so quickly. She was happier and more relaxed since she knew she would have plenty of time after work and on weekends to do what she wanted for her career and household. Her fellow workers experienced her as changed: much friendlier and easier to get along with. By the time she finished school and was ready to quit her job, she felt sorry to leave. She even cried at the good-bye party for her. Her co-workers said they would miss their enjoyable friend! She applied her hypnotic skills when given the invitation to do so; great benefit for her and others resulted, helping her cope and transcend.

⌘

In this chapter you have experimented with many different hypnotic possibilities. Hopefully, you have approached the exercises with openness to your individual abilities, developing and enlarging upon these skills. Creative adjustments will help transform difficulties and resistance into assets. You can return to these basic exercises over and over. This adds to and embellishes upon the learnings you have begun until eventually trance becomes a comfortable and readily available tool.

Seven

Overcoming Resistance

I do not say that we should try, without training or experience, to explore our own subconscious depths. But we ought at least to admit that they exist, and that they are important, and we ought to have the humility to admit we do not know all about ourselves, that we are not experts at running our own lives. We ought to stop taking our conscious plans and decisions with such infinite seriousness.

--Thomas Merton

Hypnosis can be a pleasant and interesting experience, an opportunity for new learning, growth, and development. Yet, even though you want to experience hypnosis, you may find yourself unable to go into trance. In this chapter, use exercises to help you work with resistance to trance.

You have been gathering data like a scientific researcher. You may feel ready to form a hypothesis, but it is still premature to draw conclusions based on the partial information you have. Continue to set aside judgments about yourself or your experience. Instead, turn your attention to the flow of awareness, just as it is. The next exercise, drawn from Eastern meditation, shows you how to follow the stream of your awareness without conceptualizing about it.

Following the Flow of Awareness

Find an undisturbed place and relax for a few moments, but do not go into trance. Instead, notice what you are experiencing. For example, if you are sitting in a chair, do you start to notice how your body feels in the chair? Or perhaps you consider doing this exercise, then wonder how you will do it. Observe and notice each thought, as your attention roams about. If you got lost in a particular thought, return to simply following your awareness. Stay with experiencing the present moment until you feel ready to stop.

Do this exercise several times at different sittings until you can follow your awareness. What difficulties have you experienced? Has anything prevented you from successfully continuing to be aware, moment to moment? You may feel that the exercise was easy, perhaps even a bit dull. But what led you to stop when you did? Did you run out of things to notice? When did this happen? What areas were you ignoring? For example, some people do well with pointing out every object around them, and then they stop with nothing else to notice. In this case, inner experiences, reactions, and associations may be ignored or avoided, while attending only to the outer field of experience. Sometimes people avoid what is happening now by immersion in the past, or worry about the future. Try to explore your own reactions to the exercise. All of this will be useful data. Do not chastise yourself for missing areas. You learn as much about yourself by what you do not notice as by what you do notice. Everything has its place, a piece in the jigsaw puzzle of mind.

Unconscious Resistance:
Opening Your Mind to Change

People develop habitual ways of doing things. Habit in action is often associated with habits in thought. You probably have noticed this while carrying out your typical activities, such as washing the dinner dishes or driving the same route to work. There are certain characteristic patterns of thought that tend to go along with habitual activity. Some habits discourage growth and development. Other habits encourage accomplishing meaningful goals efficiently and effectively.

Following A Habitual Experience

Choose a habitual activity to follow, a specific routine that you do regularly. Try to be aware of it while you are doing it. Do not interfere with the natural flow. Simply observe and notice it, as you did in the previous awareness exercise, watching without censure or judgment as you carry out the activity. Be aware of the emotional content. Feel the sensations in your body and all aspects of the experience of doing the action.

Exercise in Exploring Your Experience

After you have chosen an activity and been aware while doing it, try recalling the activity several hours later or the following day. Think back on what you experienced. Did you have any difficulty staying with your experience at the time? If your answer is yes, you can explore it now. What thoughts or feelings floated through your mind at the time? Consider possible meanings. Do these accompanying thoughts or feelings have any conceivable connection to your experience? Follow your associations and the details of possible patterns and feelings without interfering, while you carefully observe them. Sometimes associations are peripheral and distant, almost beyond grasp. Other times the connections are clear. Be patient and alert. Follow even minute cues down interesting paths. If you are touching upon a conflict area you may feel slightly nervous or uncomfortable. Rather than simply worrying about them, consider your feelings positively, as a possible indication that you are beginning to explore something important. Resistance may feel boring, uncomfortable, sometimes embarrassing. You may have lost your train of thought suddenly, or have even forgotten to concentrate. Take note of this. You may be beginning to gain understanding about resistance to trance.

Preventing Yourself from Change

Defenses can be helpful, especially when feeling the full force of an experience could interfere with competent action. Defenses are automatically adopted to protect against anxiety and threat. During a crisis, defenses can be invaluable in helping you cope well. For example, in job situations it is usually better not to tell the boss off just because you are angry.

But when used automatically, taken for granted as the world of personal potential, defenses may limit your options. Reactions to situations become too predictably patterned to allow for creativity, excitement, or growth. This can present problems when you are trying to make personal changes, as in self hypnosis.

142

Change is facilitated by freedom of choice. Learn to use defenses for defense, when necessary to endure or cope. Don't use defenses against your better functioning.

Working with Defenses

Hypnosis is often an effective way to bypass defenses. Trance works directly with the positive unconscious and bypasses conscious ego functions like defenses. However, if you have found that you are unable to go into trance, you may be putting up defenses to trance itself. If you would like to explore this possibility, try the exercises that follow.

Identifying Defensiveness

Think about trying to go into trance. As you contemplate the possibility, what is your reaction? Do you feel vaguely uneasy, then immediately make a number of convincing excuses for not doing It? Do you think of countless reasons why you can't? Or maybe you feel like circumstances never allow you to sit down to do a trance. Do you believe other people try to prevent you from trance? Do you feel fear of trance? Insight gained from self-observation may allow you to change so that you can experience trance.

It is difficult to diagnose yourself from a book, but viewing your reaction as possibly defensive may help you question whether this reaction is the only possible reaction you could have. People often believe their defensive reactions are fixed realities that seem to just happen to them. A sense of free will or choice is not experienced. Noticing another possibility can be the opening wedge for new options to begin.

Exaggerating Your Defensive Reaction

A day or more following the previous exercise, try to go into trance. This time, if you feel the usual reluctance, try to exaggerate it. If your attention wanders, try to think of anything but trance. If you get bored, bore yourself further by deliberately doing nothing. After fifteen or twenty minutes of this, once again try to enter trance. Some people will automatically find themselves going into trance at this point. Others will not. If not, shift back to the defense and exaggerate further. There is much to learn from studying how you prevent yourself from successfully accomplishing your goals.

The Positivity of Negativity

Perhaps you have faithfully attempted to work your way through this book, performing exercise after exercise, but found that in spite of all your efforts you cannot achieve even the slightest semblance of trance. You might feel frustrated and angry at yourself, or debunked the efficacy and power of hypnosis. But have you considered the strength and self confidence expressed in your resistance? This strength, when it matures, compounded with your whole personality, can actually become a driving force for resolving difficulties.

A college woman came to us for hypnosis to lose weight. She also complained about being very forgetful: She forgot her keys, the date, or even her best friend's name! She learned to develop a deep trance. We invited her unconscious to work on these difficulties creatively, using her resources. She discovered, to her delight, that she could forget to overeat! She told us that at first, she forgot several meals, including her favorite desserts. She thought this was simply an isolated incident and could not possibly relate to her hypnotic work. But she continued to experience forgetting to eat, coincidentally at useful times. Gradually she began to recognize that what she had always considered to be a deficit and a problem could actually work for her in another context. Concomitantly, her forgetfulness with keys and other things lessened, much to her surprise! Her forgetfulness found a place. She had never thought her tendency could help her.

Once the unconscious is engaged to work in a positive way, problems may not merely be bypassed but instead can be used as assets.

Positive and Negative Exercise

If you sense that you have some negativity holding you back, invite your unconscious to make new connections for you. You may know things unconsciously, that you do not know consciously. After all, you probably did not consciously and deliberately choose to be negative or to have problems. This changes naturally and automatically, when you permit unconscious resources within to work for you.

Prepare for this exercise by thinking about some of your talents and strengths. Describe them fully to yourself. Next, consider your weaknesses and faults.. Enter trance if possible, otherwise sit quietly, wondering in general about the complex unity of the human body: how the different systems are all connected: the skeletal system to the cardiovascular and muscle systems, the digestive system, etc. Consider the interactions, the overlaps. After you have imaginatively gone through the body as best you can, relax and let your thoughts drift about whatever interests you. Then take a moment to pause and meditate on your experience.

Frames of Reference

You can accomplish amazing things unconsciously, without interference from consciousness. For this to occur, depotentiate consciousness. Awareness need not be engaged in what you are doing. You have experienced this naturally when you are, for example, daydreaming. You may not have discovered how to use this natural talent.

Allow Unconscious Knowing

How do you go from the living room to the dining room? Think of as many ways as possible. Do not read on until you have given yourself at least five minutes to ponder this question. Jot down some answers. Now analyze your responses to learn about yourself and your limitations. Vary this creatively, with your own examples.

Erickson used this exercise frequently. He would say that we can go from one room to the next in various ways. We could crawl, skip, run, some could even do cartwheels, ride a bike, or roller skate. Or we could go out the door, get in the car, drive to the airport and board a plane for Hawaii. We could spend two weeks there, relaxing and enjoying the sights, then return home, and walk in the back door, through the kitchen directly to the dining room. Did you get stuck after walking, running, or crawling? How many new ways can you think of now?

New Perspectives

Imagine a place where there are six directions. Now think of one with two directions. Once again, do not read on until you have given yourself time to think.

In Arizona where the Cliff Dwellers lived, the terrain was so mountainous that one dweller's house could be directly above another. Besides north, south, east, and west these people also had up and down, giving six directions. Modern apartment buildings can be similar.

Now, can you think of a place with two directions? Many people have been to there. One answer is on a boat. What is most important is landward or seaward. Compass directions may be used, but when it is late and you are tired, your main concern is landward! On boats, there is also an intrinsic orientation to the boat itself: port and starboard, towards the bow or stern. Perhaps you know of other orientations in other contexts that are taken for granted, with two directions or with six, or perhaps more!

Flexible Perception

Look at the figure above. Can you see a vase? Look again, can you now see two faces looking at each other? Try to see the faces and then the vase. You will only see one of these two different images at a time. In order to shift from one image to the other you must conceive of the background differently. First, to see the vase, think of the white space as background. Then to see the faces as the figure, think of the black as background. This example shows how context affects experience.

Effects of Context on Perception

Take a piece of dark blue colored paper and cut it into a three inch by three inch square. Place this on a red background and look at it. Next look at another blue square on a yellow background. You will see how different the two blues appear if you place the samples side by side and compare.

Perception is relative to context and perspective. We tend at times to take our own point of reference for granted, assuming everyone shares the same view. Our own meaning matters most, our perceptual anchor.

A favorite joke in experimental psychology pictures a laboratory rat speaking about its experimenter: "I have trained that man so that every time I press this lever, he gives me food." (Watzlawick, 1974) Is the experimenter conditioning the rat with food, or is the experimenter being conditioned to give the rat food by the rat's behavior? Interaction is reciprocal.

Creative Thinking

Thinking can be defined as, "The deliberate exploration of experience for a purpose" (DeBono 1976: 32). Students in

Western schools are taught to reason with logic. *A* follows *B* directly; one fact builds upon the next. However, logical sequence can be limiting. Thinking uses skill in perception, not just logic. Creative thinking is a skill that can be developed.

Most creative problem-solvers agree that obstacles to open thinking can be overcome. Defining a situation too early leads to narrow thinking from a limited perspective, a bias.

Lateral thinking involves a refusal to accept rigid patterns and an attempt to put things together in different ways. (DeBono, 1970: 52)

Exercise in Creative Thinking

First Combine two triangles: ▲ ▲

Did you think of a diamond? Can you think of other shapes?

Now what do you have if you combine four triangles? How many shapes can you think of? This requires reorganizing and rethinking to come up with one or more larger figures made up of four triangles.

Similarly when working with yourself, you might unintentionally develop limited, patterned ways to interpret your situation. You may have one experience followed by another that always seem to go together in a certain pattern. Further experiences are dismissed as simply more of the same pattern. People inadvertently sort their experiences into restrictive, rigid categories, then feel bored or stuck as a result. Gabriel Marcel called this, "hardening of the categories." An open attitude towards interpretation can help.

Judgment

One of the greatest resistances is passing judgment on thought by jumping to conclusions. This is not meant to imply that judgments in general are unhealthy but refers specifically to premature judgments during creative thinking. When dealing with personal change, keep an open mind to discoveries made along the way. Early conclusions are temporary, rather than final. Put them in brackets: [good] [bad] [false] [impossible].

Who Can Say If It's Good or It's Bad

Once an unhappy farmer went to the village Master to complain about his plight. He told the Master that his farm was failing. He believed everything was terrible.

The Master replied mysteriously, "Who can say if it's good or it's bad."

The farmer returned to his farm somewhat puzzled. That night a wild stallion appeared on his farm. The farmer captured the stallion and harnessed it for work. He took all his money and invested in seeds, expecting that at last he would make great profits. Then he returned to the Master. He told the Master how overjoyed he was that the stallion had come. Now he could plow twice as many fields. He expected the Master to agree.

But the Master replied, "Who can say if it's good or it's bad."

The farmer returned to his farm even more puzzled than last time. He planted the seeds and worked very hard during the following weeks. The plants grew well. He looked forward to harvesting the crops soon. Then, one night, the stallion disappeared. The farmer was crestfallen. He had spent his last dollar on the seeds. All the fruits and vegetables would rot without the horse to help him harvest. He returned to the Master lamenting the loss of the stallion.

The Master replied, "Who can say if it's good or it's bad."
The farmer returned to his farm feeling desolate. But next morning, to his great surprise and joy, the stallion returned and brought with him a mare. Now the farmer was elated! Not only would he have plenty of labor force from both horses. He would also be assured of his future because there would probably be more horses from them in the future. He rushed to the Master to tell him the wonderful news and receive the Master's blessing.

Instead, the Master replied, "Who can say if it's good or it's bad."

Next day, the farmer's eldest and strongest son was riding the stallion, harvesting the crop. Suddenly the stallion reared and threw the son off, injuring him. Now the farmer was very upset. His son, the best worker, would now have to rest in bed for months. He told the Master that his grief was boundless.

Again, the Master replied, "Who can say if it's good or it's bad."

As it turned out, the National Army came around to all the farms recruiting the first born son of every family to battle at the front lines. Because the farmer's son was injured, he did not have to go. And who can say if this was good or bad? It is possible that the son might become a war hero and a stronger person from the experience, or perhaps he would have been killed.

Judgments often put people on a roller coaster of emotion. Interpretation given to circumstances can be viewed from many perspectives. Free yourself from limiting judgments that hinder your positive potential. In order to judge wisely, take many possible perspectives into account even if it requires more time.

Choosing a Hypnotist

You can work with self hypnosis after you learn to voluntarily allow the involuntary to occur. Limitations and conscious objections are set aside temporarily for the purposes of self exploration and personal growth. Ultimately, trance is a personal experience. No one can force your experience to be a certain way. With time and regular attempts you will be able to make the necessary discoveries for trance. If you find that you still have not been able to experience hypnosis and accomplish your positive goals, you may be helped by consulting a professional. Therapeutic trance ultimately takes place within the patient, but sometimes someone who is trained to recognize and guide in hypnosis or hypnotherapy will make the difference. Often you can accomplish your goals by working on your own, but certain problems or circumstances best lend themselves to consulting a professional.

You might wonder how to know when to consult an expert. The answer lies within. You are obviously interested in hypnosis or you would not be reading this book. Experiment with the general exercises in trance and suggestion. If you find that you can readily experience trance or that after practice you begin to find your way into hypnosis, then you know that you do have the ability to experience self hypnosis without external guidance or someone to point it out to you. If you cannot make any headway with these techniques and have worked through this chapter as well, consulting a professional may help you. This does not indicate that you cannot ever work with hypnosis. If the motivation is present, you will be able to experience trance with proper guidance. You may find it helpful to work with a therapist if you feel stuck or threatened, to help get you back on track, to guide you in certain areas where you experience blocks or fears, or just for support and help with a stubborn conflict. It may only require a brief time.

Choosing the right professional is a personal matter. Find a good match for you. A great array of professionals who do hypnosis are available: hypnotherapists, psychologists, psychiatrists, social workers, and medical doctors. The ideal combination is a person with experience and dedication to hypnosis as well as the helping professions. It takes skill and professionalism: hypnosis is both art and science. Learning to use your own unconscious to problem solve and make changes is central. You should look for this to occur in hypnotherapy. An ally in your endeavors may be all you need for your journey to begin.

⌘

When doing self hypnosis, work patiently, giving yourself the time and space to experience as you go along. Try to recognize your responsiveness, even if it is subtle. If the willingness is there, you can experience trance and enjoy its benefits.

PART FOUR

Navigating the Sea of Life

The exercises in Part Four are designed as stepping stones, springboards of self-exploration and development using self hypnosis. Let them inspire your own ideas, associations, and resources for change.

Eight

Learning, Unlearning, and Relearning

You can know something, but not understand it, and then again, you can understand something, but you don't know what it is.

--Milton Erickson

L earning is the realization of possibility. Continuing throughout life, learning can begin in one context and be applied in another. Meaning and potential are continually evolving.

We naturally tend to perceive things in a pattern together. Without permitting our natural tendency to perceive the interacting unity among parts, learning and memorizing becomes more difficult. We seek commonality among items that belong together, to learn and respond better. Learning leads to insight, a clear perception of interrelationships, experienced as a whole, including appropriate or correct solutions to problem situations.

Individual elements unify, to become parts of a larger whole, the pattern. Consider the many theories of learning presented in this chapter as details, elements of a larger unity, a gestalt. When considered together, these many seemingly varied aspects of learning will join together with insight through your own understandings, some conscious, others unconscious, to be developed further using self hypnosis.

Generalization of Learning

Montessori learning theory (Montessori 1964) views the natural flow of growth as moving from the concrete to the abstract. Before, an object is at first an experience. Learning takes place naturally through action. Descriptive words and concepts of the experience follow. Correct concepts can be abstracted from actual demonstrations. For example, a child playing with groups of blocks naturally realizes the concept of number. Prior to learning addition tables, children learn addition by manipulating groups of simple objects.

Hypnosis helps people evolve from basic levels of experience to more complex understandings. The learner develops abilities from simple unconscious learnings. Trance phenomena can be understood and mastered best through first-hand experiencing and self experimentation. Explore the experience first. Then allow the new learnings to broaden in their effects.

Learning is mainly linking or associating ideas, according to Guthrie, a renowned learning theorist in the 1930's. Guthrie's concept, drawn from Aristotle, is echoed in modern learning theory as well. Two events taking place together in time, especially if they happen together regularly, tend to become linked or associated. We are reminded of old situations and events when we re-experience a place associated with them. We hear an old song on the radio and remember those times and how we felt. Our memories are linked. This provides a springboard for creative learning.

Creative learning takes patterns related to one context of

meaning and applies them in another context. Many creative and inventive people derive meaningful patterns from widely divergent areas of interest. Freud, as a famous example, was a great student of archeology. He considered it his second love, only surpassed by psychoanalysis. Many do not recognize how extensively his psychoanalytical theories drew from archeology. Indeed, based on his understandings of archeology, Freud helped patients reconstruct the causes and precursors of their present problem from the psychological relics of the past. Freud was, in some respects, an archeologist of the mind.

When new learning first takes place, the learning is context bound. But as a series of similar learning contexts are experienced, the rate of learning accelerates. Gregory Bateson called this phenomenon *deuterolearning*. For example, learning your first foreign language can be difficult and take a long time. The second is learned more quickly and easily, the third is even quicker, and the twentieth is very rapid. We not only learn what we learn, we learn how to learn as we learn.

Pavlovian Conditioning

In the Pavlovian theory, also known as classical conditioning, a stimulus which automatically brings about a certain response is paired by following it with a new stimulus, which usually does not bring about the response. An association then forms between the new unrelated stimulus and the original unrelated response. Eventually, the new stimulus evokes the formerly unrelated response. The classic example of Pavlovian conditioning is ringing a bell immediately before presenting a dog with food. The dog naturally salivates in a reflex response to food. Soon, the dog comes to associate bell ringing with food. The bell is always followed by food. Eventually, merely ringing a bell makes the dog salivate. The dog has no understanding that it can have any influence on the outcome of feeding or not. It merely learns that ringing a bell leads to food, and thus responds to the bell with expectancy, as a signal for food. If the food does not follow bell ringing regularly, for a period of time, the association tends to weaken, or to be extinguished.

Learning theorists think of troublesome conflicts as faulty conditioning that can be unlearned, forgotten, or exchanged for new learnings. This theory implies that alcoholism, overeating, smoking, phobias, and other problems are the result of faulty conditioning. For example, people afraid of snakes have learned to associate snakes with anxiety. Whenever they see a snake, they feel anxiety and fear. Overeaters associate food with stress; they go to the refrigerator when they feel nervous. Successful treatment methods in this approach require that the patient regularly experience the problematic stimulus e.g. alcohol, food, snakes, etc. without permitting the usual behavior to follow, or else pairing with a different response altogether.

Opinions differ widely whether reconditioning is enough. Analytical therapists believe resolving conflicts is necessary: Therapy should work on the deeper motivations and conflicts. Most theorists who subscribe to the analytical approaches believe that change is impossible without working through the deeper level conflict. Their rationale involves a tension reduction model of problems. Conflicts cause tension; conflict and tension are expressed symbolically in symptoms like overeating, phobias, and other problems. Thus it is important to deal with the underlying conflict that fuels the symptom with energy and meaning.

Research on the outcome of psychotherapy does not consistently support the superiority of any one method or approach in all circumstances for all individuals. A balanced treatment regime that takes the individuality into account is probably best. Treatment works better when people feel hopeful and positive about the techniques. Research in outcome studies does indicate that self-selection of the treatment method leads to better results in achieving therapeutic goals. (Frank, et. al. 1978, 172-3) Thus, this book presents several methods for working with difficulties so that you use what is best for you.

Creative Applications of Learning Theories

Preventing a Response to a Stimulus

Guthrie described methods for preventing a response to a stimulus. (Guthrie 1935) One approach is to present the stimulus at a low intensity so that the stimulus does not tend to evoke the response. Then, gradually, the stimulus intensity is increased while carefully ensuring that the threshold of response is not reached. Tolerance develops.

Preventing Response to a Stimulus

For example, if you want to get used to cold showers, don't start by taking an ice cold shower. Begin the shower at a comfortable temperature. Then, turn the hot water down a little at a time, over a lengthy period. Gradually increase the duration of cold until, after numerous showers, you get used to it.

Another method is to present the stimulus cues while at the same time preventing the response from taking place by distraction with some other stimulus. For example, our clients during their hypnosis sessions, were unaware of loud, continuous construction noise next door even though most of the conversation was overshadowed by these extraneous sound. They were surprised when we mentioned the background disturbance after the session. Relaxing and concentrating on inner concerns led to our clients' unawareness of disturbing stimuli. They experienced no discomfort. Following treatment, they developed tolerance to distracting sounds in general. A desensitization process took place. They discovered an ability to spontaneously tolerate discomfort and distraction. Based in these discoveries of possibilities, these clients established new habits of response.

Many other creative uses of learning theory methods can be applied in hypnosis. Experimentation is the best way to find applications. Later applications chapters interweave these principles with trance.

Reinforcement and Frame of Reference

Educational psychologist and founder of instrumental conditioning, Edward L. Thorndike (1874-1949) developed the concept of rewards, he called satisfiers, and punishments, he called annoyers to bring about learning. When teaching a behavior, reinforcement is presented after successful performance. Behavior that approaches the requested behaviors is rewarded consistently until a connection is made between the learning pattern and the reinforcement. Subjects learn that their efforts can bring rewards or their absence. Satisfiers tend to strengthen a response, and annoyers tend to weaken or discourage the response, although Thorndike believed that punishment is not as effective as reward to bring about learning.

LEARNING, UNLEARNING, AND RELEARNING

We learn best what we enjoy and like.

These learnings remain in context. The learning situation includes ways by which the situation is defined. The context becomes a mental set that tends to bring about a certain response. Rats put in a maze repeatedly come to recognize the maze. They have learned to run through from start to finish, and not just sit there. The situation is a learning or problem-solving situation, and the rat is expectantly oriented soon after being placed there.

The way a situation is defined becomes what we have earlier referred to as the frame of reference. After regular repeated learning experiences, a frame of reference for that learning situation is taken for granted. When put in other, similar kinds of puzzle boxes, the rat gets quicker to respond by appropriate behavior. The rat has learned how to learn.

As you learn, you also learn new frames of reference that help you learn how to learn. By creative learning, you learn to transcend one frame of reference to discover a new one. For example, house-framing carpenters incorporate a point of view in their trade: speedy assembly of framing members, studs at 90 degrees with definite spacing. They work rapidly with certain tolerances for gaps and accuracy. These assumptions would not be appropriate for fine cabinetmaking where meticulous exactness and smooth finishes are expected. Even though both construct with wood, each learns a point of view during the process that becomes taken for granted.

Expanding your point of view to another area is valuable. You can achieve different results. To continue the example, if a cabinetmaker originally learned framing, he might incorporate ideas drawn from house designs and the spacing of wall studs into his furniture pieces, adding ease of installation, subtlety of textures, appropriate shapes, finish, and so on. Change involves shifting the point of view so that new possibilities can emerge from the old learnings related to a new context.

The point of view we take affects what we learn as well as our options to use what is learned. For example, teachers who are arrogant and condescending may unintentionally and indirectly give a certain frame of reference to their students that may interfere with students' performance. Some students may be threatened by this attitude toward them, becoming insecure. Others may identify with it, admiringly. Still others may manage to separate the subject somehow from the teacher, and find a rationale to explain or cope with it. Years later, when relearning or using the subject as an adult, these people might recall the context in which it was learned. Memories of the teacher can spring to mind, interfering once again. Using hypnosis to activate other experiences in related subjects, the original learning context may be transcended to a new and better one for performance. When context is transcended, a new, more comprehensive context is created that includes more possibilities for meaningful action.

Using Learning Theory for Change

Learning how to learn is essential to self help. Being interested and imaginatively involved improves learning ability. Deep immersion in learning for school or work, for example, permits rapid, effortless memorization and retention of material, as well as easy accessibility to the information. We have all had a time when we became enthralled with learning something taught by an inspiring, wonderful teacher. We found ourselves personally identifying with the material. Getting a high grade or being applauded for excellence in performance became

164

secondary to involvement. Paradoxically a high grade may have followed easily. Just to learn or do something can be intrinsically rewarding. Search for the inner value of learning itself.

In the following exercises pick a minor behavior you would like to change. Allow yourself to become fascinated with the process as you experiment with enhancing your learning abilities.

Choose a sequence of action you would like to improve in yourself. For example, we will describe working on being more organized in the household. Your usual approach to this might be to vow that you will be more organized and have a period of time in which you show improvement before you slip back to your old ways. During the time you are involved with this exercise, do not make any special efforts to organize your house. Instead, go to a bookstore or library and look at books about being organized. Think about the different ideas. Next, visit a friend who is, in your opinion, organized. Talk to him or her about it; ask how he or she is able to accomplish this. All the while, think about organization. Alternately, find out how a business is organized. If you do not know anyone who has their own business, ask a local store owner where you shop. After about a week's exploration of the topic, pick one area of your house to organize. Make it a small section, perhaps a drawer, a tool box, or some other limited area. As you do this, think about what you have learned. If this is successful over time, add something else to organize. If not, go back to your research. As you become more at home in learning about the topic, you will find that it becomes easier to make the necessary changes.

Expectations for Learning

Suggestion and expectation play a major part in learning. Therapists always build expectation for cure whether they recognize it or not, suggesting results. Johns Hopkins University researchers found favorable expectations were helpful in producing change and relieving symptoms. (Frank et. al., 1978)

People tend to follow expected pathways that earlier learnings have carved out, taking them for granted. "That's the way it is," they say. We had a client whose story of why he was seeking hypnosis illustrates this point. His car began to make a funny noise. He don't notice it at first. Eventually he became aware of a sound he had not heard before and thought, "Oh well, this car is getting old," and continued driving. The radiator overheated, he added water at the nearest gas station, and realized that the noise was coming from the radiator. He bought stop-leak and kept refilling the radiator whenever it ran out of water. He carried a water jug with him everywhere. He was late to three appointments on different occasions because the car overheated, and he had to stop to fill it. Finally, after months of this, he brought the car to be fixed. The mechanic informed him that not only did he need a new radiator, but he had a cracked block as well. He left with a very large repair bill and confirmation of his belief that he had a hopelessly old car. But what a price to pay for this assumption! Because he was convinced that his car was a problem, he did not bother to fix the problem at an early stage when the repair would have been easy and inexpensive. Correct anticipation would have made a difference. Hypnotherapy helped him change his future attitude.

Our assumptive world (Chapter 3) is the set of assumptions, beliefs, attitudes, and values that we have acquired from our experience of life. This assumptive world can be a valuable context from one point of view, for orienting, coping, and achieving meaningful goals. It can also serve as a constricting or negative limitation, a barrier, when the assumptions are inhibiting and narrow: "That's just the way things are," or "I can't do this."

Independent learning goes further than ordinary learning when we are freed from the momentum and inertia of limited ways of behaving and experiencing. Hypnosis can be used to transcend boundaries when needed, so that discovery of how to accomplish something becomes possible.

The Learning Task

The "task," a term used by Milton Erickson, is another way to integrate unconscious learnings into life. He used tasks as ordeals for learning. Erickson prescribed a minor change in the symptom. For example, the parents of a nail-biting child brought him to Erickson, pleading that he stop their son's nail-biting habit. Erickson agreed to help. He told the boy to bite one nail on each hand, but to leave all the others alone, and to bite his nails in front of his parents as loud as he liked, for twenty minutes a day. As a result, after the child was ordered to do the very thing he used to do in rebellion, the satisfaction was removed. Gradually the child bit less and less until he stopped entirely.

Tasks give people an experience in which they can grow. One client came to us for hypnotherapy because he was having difficulty writing his dissertation. He had been trying for months to work on it, but found that instead, he watched television for twelve hours a day and gained 30 pounds. The harder he tried to work on his project, the less he was able to do so. He went into a comfortable trance in the session and felt very relaxed when it was over. We asked him if he would be willing to do a task, the requirement being that he agree to do it before he knew what it was. We promised the task would not be harmful or dangerous in any way, and that it was related to his goal. He agreed. We told him his task: to climb a mountain. He replied that the task was an absolutely ridiculous thing to do. He had no idea how it could help but would do it because he had agreed he would. He returned several weeks later to his follow-up session, elated and visibly thinner. He reported that after his session, he was puzzled. He thought climbing a mountain could not possibly help him. However, he knew he had agreed to do it and felt in conflict. One day when he was walking across campus, he saw a small hill and decided that perhaps climbing that little hill would satisfy our requirement well enough. In the middle of climbing, he was suddenly struck with a realization: This was exactly what he had done with his dissertation! He had always thought his dissertation would represent the culmination of his years of graduate study and would be on a certain topic which had always interested him. But when the time came to choose his topic, he decided the original idea would be too time consuming. Instead, he opted for an easy topic that he could finish quickly with minimal effort. But when he tried to do it, he disliked the meaningless quality of the project. He took on the mountain by changing the topic back to his original choice, finding it easy to work hard on his dissertation every day.

This example shows how our client's unconscious knew

exactly what he needed to do. However, he had been unable to access this information by traditional methods. Sometimes the unconscious can help if given a situation in which it is free to make discoveries. This is the purpose of the task, a very applicable tool for self hypnosis. We encourage you to view the exercises in this book as learning opportunities. In this exploratory atmosphere, you can make many practical discoveries. A task can be more valuable than it seems.

You can have a positive interaction with your own mind, almost like an inner dialogue. Permit your unconscious to speak to you even as your conscious mind has its influence. The interaction between conscious and unconscious, within the whole person, working as a unity, brings about change. Your conscious can learn a great deal from your unconscious. You can also learn unconsciously, out of awareness. Consciousness is not always necessary. Hopefully the exercises and theories presented can help you gain respect for all facets of your mental functioning. You do not need to know what or how. Just be one with your nature.

Unconscious Learning

Both conscious and unconscious understandings are integrated in a variety of ways. Erickson pointed out that it is possible to have a conscious understanding that may differ from the unconscious understanding. Erickson defined the essence of therapy to be the changes brought about within the patient, not goals or activities specified by the therapist. Integrating conscious with unconscious understandings is not primary. Indeed, Erickson believed that conscious thinking often interferes and imposes limitations on unconscious potential.

Incidental learning is an example of unconscious learning effortlessly at work. Have you ever helped someone memorize material for school by repetitively asking questions from the textbook and found afterwards, much to your surprise and delight, that you also remembered the material you were helping to teach? People learn incidentally in many realms without conscious effort. But incidental learning happens involuntarily. Self hypnosis activates these natural mechanisms for your benefit.

Erickson demonstrated unconscious orientation in his seminars as a way that we learn naturally through the unconscious. In one seminar we attended, Erickson had been speaking for some hours, spinning a multi-textured mosaic of teaching stories. Many of his students were going in and out of trance when appropriate for their personal learning. One of the women attending the seminar remained in trance, even though all the others had come out of their trances. Erickson quietly directed everyone's attention to her. We all observed her expectantly, while he subtly and indirectly encouraged her to awaken. She opened her eyes and looked around. She seemed slightly disoriented. He asked her what he had been talking about. She demurred that she had not been following his conversation, that she had fallen asleep or into trance. Erickson then asked her to recall the last thing she remembered. Gradually, he gently but confidently drew from her an almost complete account of what he had said, beautifully illustrating how accurately though unconsciously she had been oriented. The one thing she did not recall was directly related to her psychological difficulty. He proceeded to work on it hypnotically.

Patients are aware of what the surgeon says during operations, though they are in deep anesthesia. (Cheek 1959) Cheek cautioned surgeons to be careful of what they say, since patients can pick up worries, discouragement, and negative suggestions unintentionally implanted by the mechanism of spontaneous autosuggestion.

The Conscious-Unconscious Balance

People differ in the personal balance of conscious with unconscious understandings. Insight without also gaining ego strength and coping skills sometimes leads to helplessness, fears of inadequacy, and frustration. In our clinical experience, clients with this difficulty express concerns like, "I know what I'm doing, but can't seem to stop doing it," or "It doesn't seem to help me, even though I understand." They cannot control themselves and change, though they understand what they need to do or feel.

There is an old story told about a person with a phobia of crossing the street. A friend suggested that he get psychoanalysis for his phobia. Years later, he saw the formerly troubled friend and inquired whether he ever got over his phobia. "No," answered the friend happily, "But I really understand it!"

Insight may or may not be basic for all problems. In hypnosis, action and change are important. One of our clients, a woman in her early 20's, spent several years doing hypnotherapy to make major alterations in her personality. When she began, she was shy, withdrawn, afraid of driving a car, using anti-anxiety medication, and living with her parents. She went into deep trance and learned to express herself unconsciously with automatic writing. In all the time that she was involved in hypnotherapy, she never once wanted to read her automatic writing upon

171

awakening.

This client changed tremendously from hypnotherapy. After some years of treatment, she enjoyed pursuing a higher degree at school, engaging in a career, driving her own car, and living on her own. This growth and development took place unconsciously with very little conscious insight, yet she took pleasure from her many new capacities and abilities.

Sometimes conscious orientation is limited and rigid. Good and sensitive contact with unconscious processing through self hypnosis can be useful both therapeutically and practically. The unconscious has the ability to orient intelligently. A corrective emotional experience can take place in self therapy, sometimes without conscious knowledge that it is taking place.

According to Dr. John Whitehorn, the corrective experience in therapy is primary. This experience brings about therapeutic change, regardless of insight. You can learn from an experience without necessarily understanding how or why it is helpful. Conscious insight follows if it is necessary, but the change is more important. Insight may only be symbolic of the change. Many kinds of experiences can produce corrective, therapeutic effects. This may be brought about unconsciously or consciously, or in combination. Experiment with both in your own self hypnotic work. Find the way that works best for you. Do not be like the person in the story with a fear of crossing the road, who ended by keeping the fear, but really understanding it.

⌘

Learning can be conscious, unconscious, or a combination of the two. As you learn new ways of learning, the less productive habits and patterns can be unlearned, opening new possibilities.

Nine

Sports: Achieving Your Personal Best

Technical knowledge is not enough. One must transcend technique so that art becomes an artless art, growing out of the unconscious.

--Suzuki 1959, 173

Most athletes agree that sports involves more than just body mechanics. The unconscious plays a significant part in performance during competition and training. Many articles are available in sports and fitness magazines instructing athletes to think positively and concentrate well. These partially correct approaches have their limitations. Negative beliefs or conflict between beliefs affect the athlete's mind, to help or hinder peak performance. Through hypnosis these learned limitations can be bypassed to develop untapped potential. Gains occur naturally, as if they just happen. This is autonomous learning, fulfilling unconscious potential.

All athletes have competitions when they are "on." and everything flows. Compare these peak performances to other times, when the equally well prepared athlete does not perform well. What makes this happen? What separates winners from losers among equally skilled participants? Hypnosis has long

173

held the answer to these questions: their minds, affected by suggestion.

In the exercises that follow you are invited to explore your abilities and experiment with learning to perform even more optimally.

Exercise to Get Ready

Allow yourself to go into trance. Let your conscious mind think about whatever it likes, since your unconscious will be more important. Invite your unconscious to give you an experience in your body such as tingling in your fingertips, followed by lightness and movement in your hand, spreading up your arm, or perhaps a comfortable warmth or heaviness. As the sensation increases, you can become curious about the exploration you are going to begin over the next days and weeks. Wonder what it will be like to have an intuitive learning that you may or may not understand right away. Think about this without guiding your thought in any particular direction. Drift. When you are ready you can suggest that your sensations will return to normal and you can awaken relaxed and refreshed.

Pressure

Pressure cannot be controlled by simply trying to suppress concern about it. Almost anything can subtly interfere with how well you do. For example, a snide remark from an opponent at an inopportune moment may activate emotion from personal insecurities. You can can find resources in your unconscious potential to help you alter the meaning of the situation.

SPORTS: ACHIEVING YOUR PERSONAL BEST

A ballet dancer sought hypnotherapy with us for her anxiety during performances and competitions. She worked out very hard when practicing. She usually experienced her performances as uncomfortable when audience attention focused on her. Whenever she performed, her anxiety was so great that she would shake all over with tension, which was extremely embarrassing . She could not imagine ever being less nervous. In hypnosis she learned to relax completely and feel calm. She always felt relief from her symptoms during and following trance. She began a learning process. We decided together on an acceptable alternative to shaking all over. She could direct her anxiety into her little finger, which could shake intensely during her performances. Of course, others would probably not notice, but she would know. The rest of her body was free to perform well, and she could enjoy her secret anxiety subtly hidden, in her little finger. This thought amused her.

After her next dance performance she reported that she found herself dancing well, and smiled to herself about her little secret. She was the only one who noticed the trembling little finger To the judges she merely appeared to be enjoying her performance, fully at ease, which added to her high score. This permitted her to develop further possibilities for herself, both as an artistic performer and later in life, as a performer of work.

Erickson told of a professional golfer he hypnotized to reduce anxiety during golf tournaments. After treatment, the man learned to totally immerse himself in the experience, approaching each hole as if it were his first without comparison or thought of how he was playing. When he finished the eighteenth hole, he started to tee up again. Everyone asked him what he was doing. He said that he had just started. He believed he was playing the first hole. He was surprised when told that he had won the tournament. He was just beginning!

In both cases, they creatively transformed their performance in the situation. The dancer intensified and redirected her tension, thus mastering the situation. The golfer bypassed performance pressure altogether by total immersion. The result was loss of the usual concerns and self judgments along the way. Pressure can either be intensified or diminished with the help of hypnosis.

Altering Your Experience of Pressure

Allow yourself to go into a comfortable trance. Recall the body experience you had in your previous trance, and let it develop again. Once you feel deeply in trance, ask your unconscious to think about the pressured feeling you get during competitions, performances, etc. Contemplate the two stories above. The two individuals we described were able to alter the meaning of their situations. Now contemplate your own situation. Allow thoughts, images, and feelings. Suggest to your unconscious that you can make your own discovery to help you change. If you are involved in a sport like tennis, marksmanship, or golf, taking place over a period of time or for points, what would it be like to approach each point, shot, or hole as if it were the first? Or is there a unique, personally creative way you can think about your situation, so you are free to participate more fully in the moment? Is another interpretation possible, a more interpretation?

If your activity is more of a performance-type such as body-building or dance, can you allow your inappropriate tension to reduce or be channeled to an insignificant detail? Take the time to experience this or another creative perspective fully and vividly in trance. Remember that your unconscious can make meaningful connections if given the chance. Set the stage for change and step back. Wait for your unique response. It could be a mediate response, and therefore different from what you expect, yet still related and helpful. Give time for this to mature. You may be surprised with new and unique solutions to your individual situation. When you are ready, wake up refreshed and alert.

Training

Nothing can substitute for good training. Getting the most out of your workouts requires more than just physical exercise. The old adage, "You get out of it what you put into it," is a timeless truth. Sometimes athletes have difficulty motivating themselves to work hard between competitions. Trance can help you mobilize your resources for better workouts.

Discovering Motivation

Before your next workout, find a time to go into trance. Relax your body comfortably and let your mind relax as well. Think about a time when you were at your peak. Remember how you felt, how your body was ready, how well you moved and performed. Your unconscious does not understand chronological clock time that you consciously experience. Can you recall a time when you were enthusiastic during a work out as if it were yesterday, today? Or is yesterday too long in the past? Let yourself relax as you turn your attention to remembering. When you are finished, wake up, refreshed.

Motivation is important, but is individual: What is stimulating for one person may be discouraging to another. For example, after the loss in one game of a series, some people get worried and tense, sending them into a downward spiral. For others, being behind triggers an intense come-back effort for victory. A world champion badminton player friend disclosed that the secret to her many wins was fear! She was terribly afraid that her opponents were training harder than she was. She feared they would win, so she always worked out harder and more than they did! Her intense, deeply committed effort to master her fear galvanized her to stay on top for many years. Even fear does not have to be feared. Use reactions positively. Act, rather than react.

Indirect Suggestion
to Mobilize Motivation

Suggest that you have an image occur to you as you orient yourself towards trance. Let your thoughts drift for awhile. Then, can you recall the first time, when you were younger and tried to do your sport? At first it may have seemed very difficult. Can you recall how you felt about it? Did you find yourself wanting to be involved more and more? Recall your learning process. Re-experience your early enthusiasm and dwell on the details as vividly as possible. When you have considered them for as long as you want, let yourself wake up, refreshed and alert.

Mental practice enhances performance. Research shows that people can acquire nearly as much benefit from actively imagining themselves performing their sport as from an equal amount of time spent doing it. In one experiment, 144 high school basketball players were divided into two groups: one practiced physically, the other only did mental practice. The physical practice group spent their sessions actually shooting baskets. The mental practice group spent the same period of time visualizing themselves aiming and throwing successful shots. The visualizers did nearly as well in a test session as the active practitioners (Clark, 1960). Many other mental practice studies in varieties of sports uphold these results (Richardson, 1967).

Images for mental rehearsal may be visual or use other senses. For example, for you, imagining the feeling of practicing may be more vivid than the image of it. Personal experience can help you find this out. Use the method that works best for you.

Olympic gymnastic champion Mary Lou Retton told us that she always visualized herself doing her routines perfectly before she performed. Many bodybuilders cultivate imagery and metaphors to help them surpass their limits. For example, highly successful bodybuilder-actor Arnold Schwarzenegger liked to think of his biceps as mountains when he trained. He believed this helped him gain size and strength. You can try mental practice in the next exercise.

Warm Up Visualization

Go into trance. When you feel ready, imagine yourself doing your sport very well. For example, if you are a gymnast, imagine that you are doing your routine correctly. If you are a weightlifter, picture yourself easily lifting your limit. Martial artists can experience performing a perfect kick, punch, or an entire form.

Runners might imagine running effortlessly with ease. Picture as many details as you can; feel your muscles responding. Focus your attention on this and nothing else. Enjoy the feeling you get from performing your best. Recall a time when you actually did do well, and remember clearly how this felt. Compare that imaginative experience to how you usually feel when you perform. How is this different? What did you do or feel that was unique to your peak performance?

Indirect Visualization

Find a comfortable level of trance. Invite yourself to go even deeper, through counting your breathing, following a sensation in your body, or another favorite technique. Allow yourself to relax deeply, as you respond. Have you ever observed a tiger bounding effortlessly? Have you watched a cat jump smoothly or seen birds fly gracefully in patterns, perfectly coordinated? Let your mind meditate on your own spontaneous images, associations, and thoughts. You don't know where your own associations will lead you, in search for useful insights or resources. Continue until you are ready to awaken refreshed and alert.

Focus

Many people tighten all their muscles at once when making a supreme effort. But this reduces flexibility and responsiveness. Movements become slower, less efficient, and more tiring. All of this is potentially stressful and detrimental to doing your best. Correct coordinated tensing and relaxing can enhance your efficiency and smoothness, improving sports performance.

"Focus" in the martial arts involves relaxation followed by tensing of contributory muscles at the moment of impact. This leads to optimum speed and strength combined. You can incorporate this concept into any sport by deliberately relaxing unnecessary tensions and tensing only when necessary. Be careful not to tense unrelated muscles. In a tennis stroke, do not tighten your shoulders as you swing. In running keep your upper body relaxed, gracefully coordinated.

You can use simple, isolated movement patterns to learn how to control muscle groups. This technique was described by Jacobson in his book, *Progressive Relaxation* (1929). Progressive relaxation leads to full body relaxation Major muscle groups are focused on so that you can gain control.

Progressive Relaxation
to Differentiate Muscle Groups

Lie down in a place where you can be undisturbed. Scan your body with your awareness from top to bottom, noticing any particularly tight areas. You need not do anything about them yet. Start with your toes and feet. Tighten them as hard as you can as you pay attention to the sensation. Hold your feet very tight while you keep the rest of your body relaxed for a minute. Then fully relax your feet along with the rest of your body. Pay close attention to the sensation of relaxation and compare it to how the contraction felt. Remain relaxed for a minute. Tighten your feet a second time, then after a minute relax fully. Remember how your feet felt when tensed and when completely relaxed. Notice the differences. Next tighten your legs, including calf thigh, knee, front and back, but remember not to tighten anything else, then relax. Repeat twice for each body part. Move up your body: stomach, chest, back, neck and shoulders, arms, hands, head. When you have scanned through your whole body, tighten everything at once, then relax. You should feel a much greater relaxation when you let go. Tensions can be relaxed more fully with repeated practice.

Applying Progressive Relaxation to Sports

Repeat this exercise several times over the next few days. Go back over important areas. For example, if you are a runner, try tightening your quadriceps while relaxing your calves. Or tighten your legs while you relax your shoulders and back. Imagine yourself running while you do this and keep relaxed. For weightlifters, think of a particular lift, for example, the bench press, and deliberately relax unrelated areas to focus on the important muscles. Pay attention to the overall sensation of your body. There is a particular muscle set that is ideal for the bench press for you, usually with lower back slightly arched, ribcage expanded, shoulders back or forward; a readiness for the lift that you can feel. Get feedback from a training partner. Tighten your chest and ready your body to do a bench press. This kind of work can add to your muscular control, with subtle but certain effects on smooth performance and enhanced endurance.

Improving Performance with Suggestion

For some people, specific direct suggestions can have a significant effect. Before you go into trance, think about your sport and pinpoint something you would like to improve, e.g., if you are a runner, you might like to increase your pace; weight-lifters may strive to lift more weight; soccer players work on ball control and kicking accuracy, tennis players might wish to improve their backhand or serve, martial artists increase accuracy or focus. Decide upon your target to improve, then begin.

Direct Suggestion

Go into a comfortable trance. Think about your target area. Next, invite your unconscious to produce an image or a sensation to help you improve. Be willing to be open to a creative image, e.g., Tennis players or golfers could imagine that a friendly breeze helps smooth their swing, runners can imagine a huge hand pushing or guiding them along or a lightness in their legs that makes running seem effortless. A weightlifter may suggest the weight feels lighter than expected. Let your unconscious play with this idea and develop your own technique that fits what you want to improve. Enjoy an overall relaxation and then awaken refreshed and alert. Expect positive changes in performance, but give them time to take effect.

Induced Suggestion

Some induced suggestions, such as heaviness or lightness during trance may help you gain inner control. Experiment with calming your heart and breathing. Suggest to yourself that this will happen and then wait for the response. For feedback, you can measure how well you control these involuntary functions by checking your pulse or timing your breaths. During competition the ability to be optimum in these functions can be useful.

The athlete who would truly excel must surpass the limitations of method, even transcending technique itself. (Simpkins & Simpkins, 1998) Technique becomes "no technique." For mastery, you must lose yourself. Instead of expressing yourself through the sport, let the sport express itself through you. Champion bodybuilder's efforts to develop their physiques may begin from personal motivations, but ultimately, they become sculptors, shaping their muscles like clay. Techniques of martial arts practitioners may begin from a love of tournament sport or a need for self defense, but committed practitioners become peaceful and imperturbable. Artistry transcends the individual motivations as the process evolves. At a certain point the external technique is replaced by Oneness. Then "it" happens. As Herrigel wrote:

This state, in which nothing definite is thought, planned, striven for, desired or expected, which aims in no particular direction and yet knows itself capable alike of the possible and the impossible, so unanswering is its power. (Herrigel 1971, 41)

Surprisingly, higher levels of play take place when you do not consciously think of play. Instead, you permit the process of playing the sport to be spontaneous and unintentional, without concepts, words, or labels.

A Zen master named Shoju Ronin was visited by a number of swordsmen who wanted to improve their sword-play. His talk over tea inspired them, but they were skeptical. They believed their rigorous martial arts training made them superior in the world of practical combat.

The Ronin challenged them to try to strike him with their swords, while he used only a fan to protect himself. Amazingly, they could not find an opening to attack and eventually had to admit defeat. Another monk who had watched the entire encounter asked how this was possible, since the master had never practiced with a sword. Shoju Ronin answered:

When the right insight is gained and knows no obstruction, it applies to anything, including swordplay. The ordinary people are concerned with names. As soon as they hear one name a discrimination takes place in their minds. The owner of the right eye sees each object in its own light. When he sees the sword, he knows at once the way it operates. He confronts the multiplicity of things and is not confounded. (Suzuki 1959, 204)

This can be applied in a practical sense to winning and losing. Takano Shigeyoshi, one of Japan's greatest twentieth century swordsmen, stated "It goes without saying that as soon as one cherishes the thought of winning the contest or displaying one's skills in technique, swordsmanship is doomed." (Suzuki 1959, 205)

The exercise that follows is drawn from Zen meditation. Practice it daily over a period of time and you will begin to experience for yourself what Zen masters have known for centuries: Practice is enlightenment. (Simpkins & Simpkins, 1997b)

Discovering Clear Mind

This exercise is best done sitting cross-legged and upright. Close your eyes and relax. Begin by following your breathing as it goes in and out. Watch each breath and eventually you will feel calmer. Next imagine a blue sky, a clear still body of water, or a blank screen. As thoughts try to interfere, let them flow past without attaching yourself to them. Do not let yourself follow the train of thought; simply notice it, let it pass, and return to the image. Finally, let your image pass. Stay with the emptiness. Do this with any distraction that comes up: outer sounds, or inner feelings, thoughts. Always return to clear mind. Repeat this exercise often. You will find that it becomes easier to clear your mind of thoughts. After you are comfortable with the exercise, try it while performing your sport. Let your body move without deliberate thought. Maintain your calm.

⌘

Using self hypnosis, higher levels of skill become possible when body and mind act as one. Months may be spent in deliberate, thoughtful training to prepare for a contest. But at the actual point of performance, transcend technique and allow actions to flow naturally of themselves. This is what Zen Buddhists call "no-mind." Thoughts or feelings do not hinder the free performance of what has been mastered. You cannot help but do your best, for no other way is before you.

Ten

The Path to Self Control

*On the occasion of every accidental event that befalls you,
remember to turn to yourself and inquire what power you
have for dealing with it.*

--Epictetus

Hypnosis can be very helpful for difficulties with self control such as overeating or impulsive behavior. People who have these difficulties may be aware of indulging but feel compelled. This often leads to a negative feeling of being out of control. This chapter will discuss ways to regain control of impulsive behavior, using weight loss as the primary example. Most of the principles may be adapted to other goals with appropriate variation.

Anyone considering a weight loss program should always check with a physician to ensure that there are no medical problems. Changes in weight can be due to many factors. Check with your doctor. If no physical complications are found, the only obstacle to change is your own mind.

Will power is not the determining factor in losing weight. Even with the best of intentions, dieters are subject to the law of reversed effort. The more you try to diet, the more you think about food! Instead, enlist positive unconscious functioning to accomplish goals. Awareness and proper attitudes set the stage; suggestion and hypnosis offer tools.

Getting Started

Begin your weight loss by suspending efforts to diet for at least a week. Eat as you normally would when not on a diet. Objectively observe how you normally eat. This is not an invitation to overindulge. Let your natural tendencies emerge. What happens? Don't try to change yet. Notice how you experience eating, and what your eating patterns are. Keep a journal if you would like.

Balancing Your Diet

Get information on nutrition and proper diets. Become highly informed about food and its effects on the body. Check authoritative sources. Consult recognized experts if necessary, to be accurate. Your doctor may have useful pamphlets. Public libraries are excellent resources. Certain sports or activities may have special nutritional requirements as well. Include your own understandings and wisdom.

After you have gathered this information, set up a well-balanced diet that includes all the food groups. Some may want to use special diets that are available. Do not start to diet until you have completed your week of observation and feel ready to commit yourself fully.

Adding Exercise

Getting adequate exercise will greatly enhance your weight loss as well as your health. Research the benefits of exercise. Learn more about how often is best and what types are best for you. If you are inactive, consider adding a fifteen minute walk each day. If you already exercise, try to add a little more time or intensity to your workouts. Be moderate in your changes, but do them.

Erickson once treated an overeating client by requiring that she only buy enough food for one day at a time. Each day she was to walk to the grocery store and purchase her food for that day only. This demanded an absolute commitment to the process and extra time, a test of her resolve. If you are willing to do this, it is a good way to prevent your consuming excess food and enlist your personal cooperation with the interesting process you are about to begin.

Not Tasting

Many dieters will claim they are overweight because they love the taste of food. However, overweight people often consume food so quickly, they taste their food less than they realize, and consequently do not get satisfied. Learning to slow down, taste, and experience food can be helpful for overcoming weight problems. It takes time to realize you are full. Developing sensitivity to taste can help get you back on track.

Taste Analyzer

Choose a food to taste. Rate the food in terms of each of the following elements, from least (zero) to most (10)

Sweet   0 1 2 3 4 5 6 7 8 9 10

Sour	0 1 2 3 4 5 6 7 8 9 10
Bitter	0 1 2 3 4 5 6 7 8 9 10
Salty	0 1 2 3 4 5 6 7 8 9 10

Circle the appropriate number for each of the four categories. Do this for your favorite food, a food you like, and a food you dislike. Make up a taste card for each food and try many different foods. Add a brief description at the end of the taste card with the following categories: consistency, color, appearance, temperature, and degree of liking, from 0-10 (Bruno 1972, 96-8). You may like to try this with friends or family.

Changing Habits

Observe your eating habits. People who habitually overeat usually indulge at a certain time of day or night. For some, a particular food triggers overeating. One client would feel compelled to eat an entire gallon of ice cream after she had her first spoonful. Another client was surprised that she gained weight from healthy foods like granola, fresh baked whole wheat bread, and pasta. She never ate any junk food, but admitted she overindulged in healthy foods. The quality of food was high; the quantity led to her problem. Habits are learned, and therefore can be unlearned.

Observing in Trance

Go into trance. Imagine watching yourself eating, as if watching in front of a mirror. What do you observe? Try imagining yourself eating at different times of the day including late night binges and early morning breakfast.

Exploring Eating Habits

Notice whether you eat in reaction to something, such as when over-tired, under stress, nervous or worried. Do you have certain foods, times of day, or other events that lead to overeating? Observe and learn about your assumptions and consequent behavior. Remember not to pass judgment on your actions. You may discover that you have a reason for your troublesome habit, an explanation or belief that seems reasonable in your assumptive system.

After you have made observations of your pattern, consider the following: Do you need to change your habit? Do you really want to change? Do you actually believe you can? Answer honestly. Only you really know the true answer. Only you need to know the answer. But the answers to these questions are part of your basis for changing your habit.

Symbolic patterns, like overeating, are often taken for granted as the constant, inevitable world of the sufferer, trapped in assumptions and beliefs of unchangeable circumstances. Hypnotherapy can be an effective means to overcome this. A new perspective appears, and with it new beliefs arise. Assumptions can change; conflicts can resolve. Behavior will reflect the change as self control becomes natural.

Working With Your Unconscious Mind

Conscious insight may help to uncover the source and meaning of self destructive patterns. But inner change must also take into account your intuitive, unconscious side. Intuition is an essential component of true insight (Reik, 1948). Insight should includes alternative solutions.

Setting Yourself for Change with Trance

Permit yourself to go very deeply into trance. Let your breathing become steady. As your trance deepens, invite your thoughts to clear. You can let go of unnecessarily tense muscles, perhaps by visualizing a peaceful place where you can be calm and at ease, now or in awhile. Follow your spontaneous response. Do not try to force yourself to be calm. As you feel calmness develop over time, you can begin to have confidence in your ability to relax and be calm in general. This calm, confident feeling will increase, gradually becoming an expected part of your life. Let this deepen as you relax fully. When you are ready to awaken, suggest that your sensations can gradually return to normal. Wake up refreshed and alert. Repeat this exercise often.

Ideomotor signaling is one way to communicate using unconscious response. You can learn a great deal unconsciously, if you listen. Listening to your unconscious guides you to better understanding of your difficulty. Review the ideomotor signaling exercises in Chapter 4, then try this one.

Ideomotor Signaling
for Unconscious Response

Go into a deep trance. Make sure you are sitting or lying so that your hands are free to move. Assign one hand as "yes" and the other as "no." Let your thoughts drift around some of your new learnings regarding your eating. As you permit this, allow yourself to go more deeply into trance. When you feel ready, ask yourself whether your unconscious understanding agrees with your conscious understanding. Wait for the response in one of your hands. You can check on some of your other understandings of yourself in this way. You may have an intuitive sense. If you have learned and responded well, you have begun to develop inner rapport.

Trance offers opportunities for discoveries that will help you along your path. The following exercises offer some direct and indirect weight loss suggestions. Consider your own individual needs, beliefs, and resources for suggestions that will fit you. You may use what is given in the exercise directly or vary it.

Weight Loss Suggestions

Go into trance and try some suggestions that can make your weight loss easier. For example, if you overindulge in chocolate, do you wonder when you will want less chocolate? At times, do you forget about chocolate? Aren't you curious what it would be like without this urge? If you tend to eat at night, could you ever feel less hungry and eat less at those times? Are you ever too busy to eat, or maybe too tired? Do you have other creative ideas of your own? Use these suggestions as springboards to your own positive ways to help you lose weight. You have resources you do not know you have. You must seek them within.

Sometimes you know things but do not consciously understand them. Unconsciously you can access subtle intuitions and other data. By allowing associations and the flow of thoughts, feelings, and memories in trance, positive unconscious processes are freed to make connections, learn, develop and help bring about change.

A woman requested hypnotherapy for a problem with overeating. She was a cashier at a restaurant. She complained of feeling vaguely bored with her life. She passed her breaks eating one delicious, discounted snack after another. She spent much of her working time thinking about what she would be eating next. She enjoyed going into trance and discovered she could relax deeply. Through unconscious analytic exploration of meanings, she realized she was unhappy in her life. In a symbolic sense, instead of fulfilling herself in life, she was filling up with food. She was an intelligent woman who was actually interested in many areas of learning, but had not permitted her wonder and curiosity to be satisfied. Snacking did not satisfy her true hunger. After she realized this, she started to read during her breaks instead of snacking. As time went by she became less and less interested in overeating, eventually went back to school, and now pursues a profession, truly fulfilling herself.

Indirect Weight Loss Suggestions

Go into a relaxed and comfortable trance. Review your trance learnings, which you may or may not need to consciously remember afterwards. Wonder about how your body integrates as a unity. Do you know how the bones, muscles, and internal organs are all connected? Even if you do not know, you can make connections and find solutions. You may have intuitive unconscious surprises, new attitudes, or different perspectives. This becomes possible if you permit your inner light to shine.

Impulse Control

Impulse control may be related to overeating. In order to diet, a certain amount of control over impulses is extremely helpful. Overeaters feel compelled, believing they are helpless to do anything about it when they desire to overeat. Trance gives opportunity for a new experience of potential.

Impulse Control in Trance

Use your favorite method to enter trance. After you have achieved a comfortable trance, let your attention drift. Suggest to yourself that gradually you will develop an itch. It might be in your arm, leg, or face. As it increases in intensity, try suggesting that you can also have a corresponding counter impulse, not to scratch. The more it itches, the less you will want to scratch. Do not scratch. As you relax the itch weakens. Suggest to yourself that with every breath the itch sensation will diminish until it is completely gone. Imagine a pleasant unrelated memory, or perhaps just forget about the itch altogether. Experiment. Try different methods until you find the technique that works best for you. After a few minutes, if you are on the correct path, the itching sensation will subside, until it totally disappears. Continue to relax. Stay in trance for a few more minutes. Then wake up fully alert and refreshed.

Trance can be used to help alter a rigidly fixed self concept. The following exercise will help you accept and feel more comfortable with change.

Altering Your Image Unconsciously

Invite yourself to go deeply into trance by imagining a profound sense of relaxation in your muscles. Your hands and feet may tingle and begin to feel light. The lightness in your hand begins in your fingertips. Can they become so light they want to raise? The feeling can move into your hand and up your arm until your whole arm raises. As you become more and more comfortable, imagine your body becoming a few pounds lighter. Enjoy how this feels. Continue to feel yourself getting lighter: one pound lighter, five pounds lighter, then ten, in small increments until you reach your goal. Feel this vividly and enjoy the experience. You can vary this exercise by using pictures and images instead of sensations. See yourself becoming thinner and thinner in a mirror. Notice how natural and comfortable this looks.

When people have a difficulty, it is often an incomplete attempt at problem resolution (Rossi, 1968). All of the different components of a problem are important expressions of the personality, even the rejected or repressed parts. Both sides of a conflict need resolution: the impulse and the counterforce to it. For example, potential for positive aggression, in the sense of taking action to accomplish personal goals, can be bound in repressed anger and frustration. It needs to be transformed. An illustration of this point is the case of a woman who came to see us for hypnotherapy to lose weight. She was outwardly placid, kindly, and extremely moral. She often did things for others before thinking of herself. But she was uncomfortable inwardly. Others could sense her deep inner tensions and frustration.

As her hypnotherapy progressed, she felt great waves of suppressed anger surge and wash over her in trance. She did not understand or know the source, at first. With time, she recognized that she was angry about many unresolved conflicts. This put her in a bind, since she believed anger was wrong. She was not able to come to terms with her opposed feelings and judgments. She needed to mature to allow her primitive anger to transform. These seemingly negative emotions and attitudes were potential assets, though understandably, her anger was unacceptable in the form it appeared to her conscious mind. Through trance work she was able to feel and express many things. As she accepted her own deeper feelings more completely, she became less angry and more tolerant of others. Her reactions found a mature equilibrium as she came to terms with her inner feelings.

Accepting Yourself in Trance

Go into a very deep trance. Invite your unconscious to experience one of the trance phenomena you have done successfully before. Recall the positive experiences you have had in trance, like a calm, comfortable feeling. Enjoy the experience. Encourage your unconscious to be supportive and helpful. You can allow this part of you to strengthen and develop. As you become more comfortable with trance learning, you will find that you can become more comfortable with yourself and all your varied aspects. Let your thoughts drift about this and continue to relax deeply. How long after trance can you feel more comfortable about yourself? Will you be more accepting immediately or perhaps in a few days? Do you feel more positive in the morning or in the evening, at home, when you are tired but at ease, or at work? Are you more comfortable when you are with family, friends, or alone? What positive potentials do you have? Do your friends and family see more potential in you than you see in yourself? You may have undeveloped potential, unrecognized as positive in how you interpret it. When you are ready, awaken refreshed and alert.

⌘

Use hypnosis regularly. Daily trances are best. Do not chastise yourself for slips--simply go on from there. Like the golfer who played each hole as if it were the first, you can lose one pound at a time. Change of habits is important. Gradual weight loss is best, giving you time to form healthy eating habits permanently. Monitor your progress, and do not avoid support in this endeavor.

Eleven

Beyond Pain

It is painful
To gain release
Enter trance
Then pain will cease

--C. Alexander Simpkins

To many people, pain is an uncomfortable sensation that cannot be escaped or controlled. Somehow, pain must be endured until it passes. But pain is an experience with a subjective aspect. You can make a difference, take control, and alter your perception of pain. You have had times when you have been very uncomfortable, perhaps during an illness or grief from a personal loss. If you were playing a competitive game or trying to meet an important deadline at work, you might not have noticed the discomfort until you stopped to rest. Then suddenly, it hit. The pain surprised you, and you thought of nothing else. This natural ability to disregard discomfort commonly occurs when a more compelling stimulus fills the mind. The inner subjective quality of pain makes it conducive to alteration using hypnosis.

History demonstrates that hypnosis has been used successfully for many kinds of pain. Applying hypnosis to controlling severe pain requires skill and deep focus of attention.

These mental tools can help you endure inescapable discomfort.

Sometimes hypnosis can be used when heavy medication is not advised due to reactions to it. One client had recently overcome a problem with drug abuse. She was about to undergo a nasal operation and was afraid she might return to drugs following surgery. She decided to try hypnosis as an alternative to medication. She learned to go into trance two days before the surgery and practiced a second time the day before. Immediately following surgery, we visited her in the hospital. She was having severe pain and felt very frightened. With permission, we induced a trance. She relaxed noticeably all over and regained her positive attitude. Upon awakening she felt so much relief she could touch her nose slightly without any pain.

Several days later we saw her again. She stated that she had a strange experience. Her husband was skeptical about using hypnosis, and convinced her the time she spent relaxing and doing trance was unnecessary. Why not just take a pain killer? She decided to follow his advice and tried a codeine pain control medication that had been prescribed. Much to her surprise, the medication did not stop the pain as effectively as hypnosis, and she suffered from uncomfortable side effects. With the confidence gained from her sessions, she was able to resist returning to abusing drugs. She decided instead to recommence using self hypnosis for the pain, and attained immediate relief. She also liked the feeling of self control she gained. Hypnosis can be a powerful analgesic whether the subject totally believes it will work or not. But the subject must be prepared and willing to try it.

Hypnosis has been used successfully for control of severe cancer pain. Barber (1980, 131) states three succinct advantages

200

for using hypnosis in cancer pain control. Hypnosis can alleviate pain without destructive or unpleasant side effects. Relief can range from moderate control to total analgesia. This can be accomplished with no reduction of normal functioning or mental capacity. Furthermore, people do not develop a tolerance to hypnotic effect as they do with many pain relieving drugs. Instead, hypnosis promotes life-enhancing attitudes, and beneficial changes in attitudes toward cancer. When combined with regular medical treatment, hypnosis can act as a supportive, positive help when enduring unavoidable severe pain.

In some cases pain serves an important purpose, such as when children slightly touch a hot stove and experience the pain of a potential or minor burn. Were it not for feeling pain, they might not learn the danger of touching hot objects. Since pain serves a protective and warning purpose for the body, you must be cautious about simply obliterating pain signals in all cases. However, the severity of pain in some instances may interfere with functioning, so pain can be diminished without harm. When working with severe pain in self hypnosis it is important to coordinate with your physician or psychologist, so that you do not mask a condition you should attend to. Always check first.

Methods for Pain Control

There are numerous techniques for pain control. We will present a few of the most effective methods with examples. Usually, one simple direct suggestion is not as effective as complex groups of indirect suggestions. Use the exercises in combinations. Experiment to find what works best for you.

Hypnotic Modification

This approach combines pain sensation with other suggested sensations such as tingling, warmth, heaviness, or coolness. You have experienced these sensations from exercises in earlier chapters. Again, we want to emphasize, do not alter pain without checking it out with a doctor. Pain is a warning signal. Find out what it means before trying to change it. Your body may need care. If pain must be endured while you are treating the condition, or if no treatment is necessary or possible, then use these methods.

Hypnotic Modification Exercise

Though you are highly aware of and bothered by your discomfort, you can allow yourself to relax somewhat and find as comfortable a position as you can under the circumstances. Let your hands rest at your sides and notice whether you could begin to feel an interesting sensation occur there. Let this develop into a feeling of warmth, tingling, heaviness, lightness, or whatever you would like to feel. Now as you pay attention to this feeling, intensify it and allow it to spread. As it spreads, does it begin to move over the area of discomfort, altering the experience? You can have a variety of possible sensations. You might feel warmth, tingling, lightness, or heaviness. Your body could feel close or far away. Wait for your experience to develop. Give yourself time.

Diminution

Sometimes pain can be intense but manageable with hypnosis. A female patient had recently undergone dental surgery, and her dentist gave her the option to take codeine following surgery. She did not like the grogginess she felt as a side effect from codeine, but was afraid of the pain she felt without the drug. She decided to try hypnosis instead and wished to begin immediately during a party her sister was having at her house which we were attending. We went into a quiet room and invited her to begin. She developed a light trance, stating that she did not feel like much was happening. We asked her whether her unconscious knew the difference between feeling her pain fully and feeling one percent less pain. Such distinctions might be difficult to notice, but we hoped she would make minor adjustments here and there. She awoke from trance and said it felt a tiny bit better, but not much.

Throughout the evening we watched her behavior change. At first she sat in a corner with a pained expression. As the evening wore on she gradually began to chat with people who walked by. Several hours later she was standing, smiling, and talking comfortably. When we asked her, she said that the pain had subsided ever so slightly at first, but after a while it was better and better, until almost gone.

Diminishing Pain

You can experiment with this kind of suggestion in trance. Invite your unconscious to imaginatively compare the difference between feeling your pain fully and feeling one percent less. What is the difference between 99% pain and 95% pain? Wonder how your unconscious could lessen the pain. How does it? Would it be a gradual process of not feeling or would a different, more comfortable feeling take its place? You may be curious how long it would take to become pain-free. Remain in trance as you think about these things. Then, awaken and allow your own unconscious to help in whatever mysterious way it wishes. You don't need to know how the pain disappears, or where it goes.

Dissociation from Pain

You can be free of discomfort by distancing yourself from the sensation, as if watching the uncomfortable feeling from far away. Many people have had the experience of leaving difficulties behind while taking a vacation. Upon return, the unsolved problems seem less overwhelming. This is an everyday form of dissociation. Take a vacation from your pain.

Erickson's patient felt faint whenever her surgeon changed the dressing after surgery. Erickson taught her to use her mind creatively with hypnosis. She said to her doctor:

"You know very well, Doctor, that I always faint when you start changing my dressings because I cannot endure the pain, so if you don't mind, I will go into an hypnotic trance and take my head and feet and go into the solarium and leave my body here for you to work on." When the doctor was gone she returned with her feet and head to rejoin her body, feeling quite comfortable. *(Erickson 1980, 243)*

Exercise in Dissociation

Go into trance. Imagine watching yourself going into trance. You can do this by picturing how you look as you begin to feel your trance develop. You can imagine looking at yourself in a mirror. You could actually watch yourself in a mirror if you cannot visualize it at first. Then close your eyes. Watch as you let go of tension. See your muscles settle, your facial expression smooth out as you release unnecessary tensions in your mouth, jaw, eyes, head, neck, and shoulders. As you watch carefully, you begin to be aware of yourself watching yourself. Where are you watching from? Are you above, far away, at the beach, in the woods, watching television or a movie of yourself in trance? Be creative and enjoy the feeling of distance. When you are ready, go back to your body and awaken, relaxed and refreshed.

After you develop skill in dissociating, time offers new resources. In progressive illnesses, people can temporarily feel better and cope better, if they regress to a time when the illness was not so severe, or even before the illness began. Your memory can be a wonderful source of positive feelings. If the circumstances of your life require that you confront painful or uncomfortable adversity, recall your own resources from the past for help. Then, you may grow in strength of character, as you endure your pain with dignity.

Dissociation in Time Exercise

Vividly recall how you felt yesterday, your sensations, thoughts, and feelings. Yesterday, the day before yesterday, last Thanksgiving, two birthdays ago, are as vivid as today to the unconscious. Search back to a time, perhaps last summer or a particular holiday, for a nice, pleasant experience you enjoyed. Now return to a time before the illness or pain began. Invite a clear memory that will become that moment now. How did you feel when pain-free? Re-live it now. Can you vividly imagine your experience and how you felt, as if here and now? Sometimes this begins with a partial memory. Accept what you are able to recall, as the basis of further developments. Keep this with you, a resource to use whenever you need it.

Applications for Pain Control

As has been shown, hypnosis can be used for pain control in many areas. Obstetrics and surgery are two areas where hypnosis has been widely and successfully applied as well. You can also experiment with hypnotic techniques to help with pain from headaches.

Obstetrics and Surgery

Childbirth and surgery are excellent opportunities to use hypnosis. Motivation is very high for a successful effort, and attention tends to automatically focus on this significant event. Even if hypnosis cannot be used exclusively during the operation, it can be helpful post-operatively, reducing the need for medication while helping with the recovery.

A woman requested hypnosis from us to help her prepare for the birth of her second child. Nine years had passed since her first, very painful delivery. She felt extremely apprehensive of the second. She began weekly sessions during her seventh month of pregnancy. She entered a deep trance, then imagined a cabin in the mountains by means of vivid hallucination. She felt as if she were actually in the cabin as well as in the room with us.

206

Whenever she thought of snow, for the purpose of therapy, she entered deep trance.

Finally, during one of her sessions she returned to the experience of her first birth. She watched the entire process as a little mouse in the corner of the room. She noticed many decorative details, such as the color and pattern of the wallpaper and the sound of the doctor's voice. Although she could see herself lying on the bed in pain, she also noticed herself experiencing the wonder and beauty of the birth experience.

Upon awakening, the client remembered everything. Now she realized she had many positive feelings during her first childbirth. Before, she only remembered the pain. She discovered a new, more creative and positive interpretation of childbirth. She was grateful for her new perspective.

We gave her a little stuffed mouse as a gift for the baby. She brought the stuffed animal with her to the hospital. Whenever she felt pain from a contraction she thought "snow" and was able to delight in the birth process while being relaxed at her little cabin in the mountains. Her second experience was not painful.

When using hypnosis for childbirth or for surgery it is helpful to prepare ahead of time. Practice for childbirth should ideally begin around the seventh month, every week up to the birth. When undergoing surgery, practice with trance phenomena and suggestion during several sessions ahead of time. Try many different approaches and pay close attention to autonomous, natural response. Your strong motivation, built into the situation, will automatically facilitate the process.

Headaches

Research over the past thirty years indicates that no single factor is responsible for causing headaches. Nor do all people react in the same way. Tension that brings about pain in one person might inspire another to accomplish more in reaction. Always ensure first that nothing is medically wrong. Headaches may be signs of dysfunction, or they may not. The following exercises are specifically designed for the headache-prone individual.

Chronic tension is a trait common to people who are prone to headaches. You can learn how to overcome a chronically tense orientation through self hypnosis. Relaxation is one factor that can help in preventing the onslaught of headaches. Relaxation techniques can sometimes replace or reduce analgesics without harmful side effects. With hypnosis it is possible to be relaxed even when you are thinking about something else. Unconscious responsiveness occurs without conscious attention.

Relaxation

Tense people often do not believe they can relax, though they wish they could. But, they have had moments, however fleeting, when they are relaxed without trying and without noticing. Perhaps it was a time with a friend, or maybe on a walk in the woods, while curled up by the fire, or after a hard workout. For example, recall a time when you did not have to do or think anything in particular. You simply were relaxed and comfortable. What was it like? This natural ability to be relaxed can be activated after trance work. Review the sections on relaxation. The exercises in Chapters 4, 5, & 6 can be helpful here. Work particularly on allowing all your muscles to relax and be comfortable. Do not force yourself to relax. Rather, let it happen. Look for any small beginnings, maybe in your eyes or shoulders, and enlarge on this response. Practice as frequently as possible, experiencing relaxation regularly in trance. By contrast you will begin to notice when you are tense during your day. Whenever you notice yourself tensing, let yourself become more relaxed as you have practiced. Relaxation will become a habit.

Another helpful ability is hand warming. People usually find that their hands become cold when they are in the midst of a headache. Warming of the extremities brings blood flow to these areas, and will increase your feeling of self control. This technique is part of meditation training.

Hand Warming

Try this exercise first when you do not have a headache. This will help you focus when you are feeling pain. Sit down and place your hands together, palm to palm. As you develop trance, direct your attention to your hands. Let your muscles relax. You might prefer to use an image of warmth, such as warm sun, or a direct verbal suggestion that your hands could become warmer, or tingle before becoming warmth. Experiment first with a direct approach. Refer to earlier chapters for more ideas. Give yourself a suggestion that you will find it easy to produce the effect under any circumstances. An indirect method might be to wonder when your hands will become warm: will it be now or later? You might want to use a key word or image to trigger the reaction. Then allow your response to take place. Practice this several times and you will find that it becomes easier.

Headache Paradox

Erickson viewed headaches in the following way:

Your unconscious can use a headache, use a bellyache, use constipation, use classical music, it can use a best seller, it can use a trip out to the park. Your unconscious is capable of using so many things, either for your profit or for a loss. The headache is a loss. (Haley 1985, 67)

Consider a headache from this larger perspective, and change becomes easier to envision. People who suffer from chronic headaches usually have them for good reason. It might seem paradoxical that anyone could have a good reason for a headache, but if you pause to think about it candidly, you may discover a personal reason for your own headaches. Erickson believed that an important question to ask is, how many headaches do you need for that reason, known or unknown? (Haley 1985, 62) How much tension and stress is optimum for you? Is this the only way? Or can you cope better, with less pain?

Lessening Your Headaches

Go into trance, wondering how fully your muscles can relax. Consider your headache patterns. How long do they usually last? Do headaches really have to last that long? How often, how severe, and how inconveniently do they strike? Is there some unknown reason for having these headaches? Could you have less headaches per month? Could your headache leave a half-day sooner? Could you have those headaches more conveniently? In other words, what is the shortest, most convenient, least painful headache that will satisfy the reason? Let your thoughts drift and wonder about these and other ideas. When you are ready, wake up relaxed and refreshed.

People with these kinds of patterns are often high achievers: intelligent, highly motivated people. These traits can be positive and helpful. However, at times we also need to set pressures aside for inner peace, even if only for a few moments. The following exercise can help you develop a comfortable image to make this possible for you. Can you allow it to happen?

Finding Peace

Lie down. Permit yourself to go into trance. Invite yourself to experience a peaceful place where you have been or can imagine going. Envision yourself relaxed, comfortable, totally away from characteristic pressures and problems. Picture yourself there, hear the sounds, feel relaxation and comfort in your body if you can. Let this comfort spread while you enjoy the leisure of the experience. Give the experience the time it takes.

Now, compare how you feel to what you felt during the peak of pain. What is the different sensation like? Can you discover ways to reduce stress if you cannot escape your situation? Can you think of your own creative variations?

⌘

In working with any recurring difficulty, it is important to be sensitive to yourself and your needs. Expect that a change in a long standing pattern will take practice. Repetition over time is helpful. You may or may not feel the results immediately. Hopefully, you will begin to make alterations in your typical ways of coping, or your attitude towards it. You can learn to meet the challenges of life with less tension, both mentally and physically. If pain must be endured, a positive attitude helps. This can affect a chronic headache syndrome or any pain problem you are trying to improve or withstand.

Twelve

Losing Fear; Finding Courage

For a peaceful meditation, we need not go to the mountains and streams;
When thoughts are quieted down, fire itself is cool and refreshing.

                                              --Suzuki 1973, 79

ears often take on such an overpowering symbolic significance that those who suffer from them, limit their lives to try to cope with the great suffering. People often not do not realize freedom from discomfort is possible for them. But of all the problems treated by therapy, fears and anxieties have one of the highest success rates: Most are curable.

Early analytic theory conceived that fear and anxiety derive from an emotionally traumatic event. The link may be direct. For example, a victim of near drowning sometimes retains a fear of water. The link may also be indirect, as in a sexual conflict represented symbolically in a fear of snakes. During World War II, a standard therapy for fears brought on by the war, known as shellshock, was catharsis. People were guided to reexperience the trauma and let out their feelings about it. Then they could let go of it. Hypnosis was often an adjunct to facilitate this process.

Consciously reexperiencing a trauma without trance does not

213

automatically lead to change. Trance work can bridge the gap between thought and action for a corrective experience to bring freedom from the grip of fear, often without conscious insight.

A middle aged woman requested hypnosis from us as an adjunct to her ongoing psychoanalysis to help with her phobia of driving. Whenever she got on a superhighway she was stricken with an intense feeling of panic and anxiety. The feelings were so overwhelming that she felt forced to pull over to the side of the road. She needed to overcome this fear since her new job required that she drive on the superhighways. She wanted very much to be able to work at this job, but her fear was interfering.

During her hypnotherapy sessions, we taught her how to produce a fairly deep, relaxed trance. She learned about the positive potentials of her unconscious and began to feel more comfortable with her inner self.

Following the third session she reported a very strange experience. She had been driving on the superhighway and waited, as always, for her fear to strike. She gripped the steering wheel in anticipation, but nothing happened! Surprised and baffled, she continued driving. She knew that she did not understand the causes or the meanings, and yet the fear seemed to be gone. She reported feeling a great deal of relief.

She told her analyst what had occurred. He was incredulous. She had overcome the fear without insight! They had a series of two-hour sessions to try to recover the "phobic material" because he could not accept that she could outgrow her difficulty without knowing why. The analyst did not realize that conscious insight is not always a fundamental component of hypnotic learning. At times, change will occur spontaneously and naturally, and can be welcomed. The unconscious can heal itself, with a corrective emotional experience, without insight. In the learning chapter we pointed out that learning is the realization of possibility. Hypnosis assists learning.

Relaxation is one important component for overcoming fears and anxiety. You can work on developing your ability to relax with this exercise. Turn back to other relaxation exercises in the book as well. Practice until you can relax in trance at will.

Relaxation Trance

If you are doing this exercise, you may be wondering how to become less fearful and anxious. To begin, you do not have to do anything in particular. Simply rest and allow yourself to go deeply into trance in the way that suits you best. Relax fully, let all your muscles settle, and allow your thoughts to drift. Develop a comfortable calm feeling. Trust your unconscious process. Invite your unconscious to have a pleasant memory, something you have not thought about for a long time. Perhaps you will picture the place, or maybe you will reexperience some old feelings or even enjoy listening to a familiar song. Evoke as vivid an experience as possible. When you are ready, let your sensations return to normal and wake up relaxed and refreshed. Where is your fear now?

Sometimes it is necessary to develop skills in trance that lead to other skills. Try to develop the ability to comfortably have a memory in trance. Once this feels natural, you will be able to use this skill to help gain freedom from the phobia.

Trance Recollections

Go into trance, and let yourself become deeply relaxed. Remember that your unconscious can be very positive and intelligent. Things are linked, one to another, as the air we breathe links us to the outer environment. Let yourself reflect upon the interrelationships and interconnections between you and your world, how you affect it and it affects you, both directly and indirectly. Now, review a significant event in your life which could be related to your difficulty. You may prefer to view the event safely from a distance, as an image, sound, or feeling far away. Let this happen like a dream that flashes through your mind seemingly in an instant. Then, bring the event closer if you can comfortably. Perhaps the meaning escapes you. Consider how a child has certain childlike learnings based on immature thoughts and feelings. As a person grows into an adult, it is possible to review these experiences and reinterpret them from a more adult perspective. You need not consciously remember or understand significant traumatic events, but your unconscious mind can reconsider important ones from a positive and more mature perspective, incorporating learnings and understandings gained through the years. Invite your unconscious to follow these guidelines, then wait for your response. When you have finished, awaken refreshed and alert.

What would you be like without your anxieties? How would things change? If you suspect that you are using your fear for some other purpose and feel that you want to change, you must deal with the problem behind the fear.

A woman was angry at her husband, but he refused to change. He also loved to fly airplanes as a hobby. In the early years of their marriage before the problems, they happily flew together. But strangely, over time she developed a fear of flying. This upset her husband, but she did not feel responsible. Her fear hurt him, but she felt helpless to do anything about it. Unfortunately, her fear hurt her too, especially when they flew on commercial airlines for vacations. She suffered far more than she would have if she had resolved her problems. After she recognized the link and used hypnosis for change, her fear diminished. They improved their relationship and once again, they flew happily together. A better relationship followed.

Briefly Letting Go of Your Fear

Go into a comfortable trance. Relax all your muscles and let your thoughts settle. You can recall the previous trance and the many learnings you had about your fear. Whether or not you consciously know the reasons, ask yourself the following question. Even if you have a very good reason for your fear, could you be without it for just one minute, or longer, one hour, even a day,? Vividly imagine this brief period of freedom from your problem. What does it feel like to be without your fear? Think about it. When you are ready, awaken relaxed and refreshed.

Desensitization

The learning process in everyday life includes processes known as desensitization and reeducation. Joseph Wolpe worked out a method widely used in behavior therapy known as *systematic desensitization* to erase a problematic habit pattern and replace it with a healthier one. The fearful person cultivates a response that is incompatible with the unwanted response.

Systematic desensitization training begins by teaching patients how to relax at will. After they have learned how to relax, they are told to imagine the least threatening stimulus they can think of regarding the fear, for example a fear of snakes. The least threatening situation begins with being a mile away from a garter snake in a pet store. Step-by-step they imagine coming closer and closer to the snake, while concentrating on remaining relaxed. When anxiety or fear begins to arise, patients pause and relax until the fear or anxiety is no longer experienced at an uncomfortable level. Then the patient is encouraged to continue until the most threatening situation can be approached one step at a time. Maintaining calm relaxation, mastery is reached. Of course, hypnosis can be used, and in principle it is difficult to say that suggestion and hypnosis are not primary in the process, since visualization, suggestion, and relaxation are involved. Erickson found in early experiments on the nature of hypnosis that carefully visualizing and imagining a simple action, such as picking up pieces of fruit, examining them carefully, and putting them down, resulted in deep trances with hallucinations. (Erickson, 1980) Wolpe states in his book (Wolpe, 1990) that hypnosis was always part of his work, assisting in his method. Pairing incompatible stimuli (relaxation with fear) was the learning principle he used for desensitization. Perhaps trance helps make it all possible. Principles of learning and habit formation synchronize well with hypnotic methods.

The next exercise works directly on the symptom, combining hypnotic relaxation and visualization skills with desensitization. The example we use is fear of water. Substitute your own fear, with appropriate variation of suggestions and conditions. This direct technique can be very helpful. Repeat the exercise, adding your own suggestions, ideas, and associations. Stimulating your own unconscious is central in self hypnosis.

Desensitization in Trance

Go into trance. Allow your muscles to relax. Warm up with a visualization exercise. Perhaps you could picture a pleasant place or recall the scene from a book. Relax and enjoy the image. Once you have reached a deep feeling of comfort, think about your fear. Begin by thinking very generally about the fear. For example, if it is a fear of water contemplate water in general, thinking about water in a distant way. Picture yourself far away from a body of water, such as the ocean, a lake, or a pool. Maintain deep relaxation and begin to imaginatively walk toward the water. The first day you may want to stop quite a distance away. If you begin to feel tense, pause in your imagery, backtrack, and reestablish deep relaxation. Continue to relax deeply, then try again. Picture yourself gradually moving closer and closer to the water, but always backtrack if you feel fear or discomfort. Take as long as you need. Hours, days, weeks, months, however long it takes. Compare this minimal time to how long you have had your fear, and would continue to have it if you left it untreated! Keep working with this fantasy until you have successfully entered the water while remaining relaxed. These learnings can be extremely helpful for altering the fearful pattern.

Repeat this exercise over several days or even weeks. Check out your reactions by thinking about water when you are not in trance and notice what you feel. You may surprise yourself. A carefully constructed hierarchy, from the least threatening to the most threatening may help you gradually face the situation and master it.

Enhancing the Process

Now that you have been working on your difficulty, you can enhance the learning that has begun. Go into trance. When you are fully relaxed, invite your unconscious to review all related thoughts and experiences. You do not need to consciously attend to all this. But you might wonder what areas seem to need attention? Be open to pursuing these findings however is best. Offer yourself the following suggestions: 1) Discomfort can diminish, it fluctuates and varies naturally, so at times, it must be less. 2) Your unconscious knows how to outgrow your problem and can communicate this knowledge in the ways that are best. 3) You may not know for certain when you will have completely outgrown the problem, but you can learn what is necessary to learn in order to benefit. Continuing to relax in trance, review the learnings you have had and allow the growth and development to continue. Then, wake up refreshed and alert, leaving matters to your own unconscious.

⌘

When working with yourself in any area, it is important to maintain the nonjudgmental attitude we discussed earlier. Give yourself the time you need to work on your fear or anxiety. Try to be consistent in your trance sessions. When people have fears, there may be more to learn and integrate, beyond the mere symptom. If you have discovered this in your explorations with trance, then hypnosis with a therapist trained in psychotherapy may help to deepen your learning process. Sometimes, the fear simply goes away, without demanding attention to deeper change. Be open to the unknown. In the empty space, courage may be found.

Thirteen

Quitting Bad Habits

Potential awaits you
Within your mind
When habit's chains
No longer bind.

--*C. Alexander Simpkins*

Hypnosis can be a very effective way to change habits. We often are unaware of the habits we engage in. People who smoke, bite their nails, or suffer from other troublesome habits, often feel they cannot control themselves, even if they want to quit. This chapter uses smoking as an example of a habit to change, but you can apply the general approach to different habits, by varying the relevant focus. Experiment with the exercises to invite the unconscious to have helpful learnings. Permit responses to individualize.

The first step in quitting a habit is to decide to stop. Smokers must make their own decision. No one can decide for them. But a decision alone is usually not enough to make the difference, except in unusual individuals. It is only the first step. Often, the opposite takes place: quitting becomes difficult, due to law of reversed effort. Paradoxically, the more smokers try not to smoke, the more they want to smoke. They become bombarded with fantasies and beliefs about how good a cigarette would taste, and eventually go back to it. They are trapped in their assumptive world. This logic applies to other habits as well. Through hypnosis, a new perspective emerges from the unconscious.

A client came to us to quit smoking, knowing she would have difficulty doing it. She knew a great deal about quitting smoking. She had done it hundreds of times! She always gave in to the craving. Before the session, we led her to a beautiful area at the ocean. She got out of her car and following us, with a puzzled look on her face. We demonstrated taking a number of deep breaths of fresh ocean air. She did the same. Then, we asked her to throw her entire package of cigarettes into the smelliest, dirtiest garbage can we could find, filled with vomit, dog manure, rotten food, and garbage. She said, "I might return to get them." We gestured toward the can and said, "Would you?" She answered, "I had better dump my ashtray too, because I might try to smoke the butts." We urged her to memorize the smell and appearance of that disgusting garbage can, and remember it whenever she felt tempted to smoke. Then we went to the office and began the session. She experienced a deep trance.

She quit that day, never to return to cigarettes. She came in for one more session about a week later. She told us that she was surprised that she had lost her craving to smoke. She realized that the function of cigarettes was important. Without her cigarettes, she needed to find a new way to relax. She learned to do so with hypnosis. A negative experience associated with a habit can facilitate letting go of it or changing it.

Readying to Quit

Read and study as much as you can about the hazards of smoking. Learn what it actually does to your lungs and body, how smoking can affect your health. Consider how much money you spend on cigarettes and what you could do with the extra money if you quit. List all of the other reasons for not smoking: probable harmful side effects, unpleasant odor, perhaps others close to you who are bothered by smoke. View video tapes available that show the horrors of a cancerous lung, slow death from emphysema, etc. These may be helpful for your reeducation. Your family doctor's office may have information and visual aids. Try your library. Becoming better informed may help you reinforce a decision to stop, if that is your choice. Learn what you can about physical consequences, to help you make a wise choice.

Uncovering personal motivations for your habit can also be helpful. A woman in her twenties wanted to quit smoking. Her doctor had advised her that smoking was bad for her health. She knew she should quit, but she felt out of control. When we invited her to enter hypnosis, she went into a deep trance. Midway through the trance she awoke with a jolt and said, "I don't want to do this!" We were surprised and asked her to search inwardly for why she awoke.

She explored what smoking meant to her. Smoking gave her an excuse to sit down and rest, to do nothing but calmly enjoy her cigarette. She felt that giving up smoking meant giving up relaxing. Her motivation to smoke was actually a very positive one: relaxation. Whenever she had tried quitting before, she always got to a point where she became so frazzled and distraught that she returned to smoking to relax. She had to learn to separate her spontaneous natural ability to relax from the learned habit of smoking that she was using to deliberately relax. A habit either serves a purpose now, or did at one time. Changing a habit may require doing something about its purpose.

A popular misconception is that cigarettes are physically relaxing. But in reality nicotine has a stimulating effect leading to increased heart rate and blood pressure. People endow cigarette smoking with personal meaning. Smoking becomes symbolic in the mind of the smoker. Actually, suggestion gives cigarettes their seemingly powerful effect. We have often told our clients who want to stop smoking, "You were not born smoking a cigarette. Whatever cigarettes do for you, you can do for yourself without them. You knew how to relax as a child and you can be comfortable without cigarettes now."

Explore Your Habit

Explore your habit. For example, pay attention to how you smoke while you are doing it: do you use your right hand or left hand? How do you light the match? Notice the automatic process of smoking. Turn your attention to how smoking makes you feel. Do you feel more sophisticated? Are you at ease with a cigarette and awkward without one? Try to become fully conscious and aware of what you usually do automatically. Attention to minute detail is helpful in accomplishing this. Take about a week to work on these exercises and ready yourself to stop smoking. Think about it, explore it, mobilize your energies toward the goal, but do not stop smoking yet. You may not be ready.

Unconscious Change

Trance can be helpful for making discoveries. Find a restful level of trance, relaxing your muscles and letting yourself have a comfortable body experience. As you go deeper into trance, imagine an inspiring scene in nature: it might be a clear sky, clean air, the smell of fresh pine trees, a beautiful garden, the mountains, or the ocean salt air. Breathe deeply and enjoy the feeling of clean air in your lungs. Relax and let your trance deepen. Allow your attention to drift around, towards whatever seems interesting. Your unconscious already knows what is relevant far better than you can imagine. Associations to important images, experiences, and feelings will take place naturally. You can have an unconscious corrective experience, without consciously knowing it. Or again, perhaps you will know it. If you attempt to anticipate or deliberately program what you will learn, you may limit yourself and thereby miss out on many interesting new spontaneous discoveries. Instead of trying to know, permit yourself to wonder what you will learn. When you are ready, awaken fully alert.

The habit of smoking is an important area to explore. Sometimes people keep smoking just because they always have. They may think themselves into a corner to justify the habit. Habit develops inertia, the tendency for a habit already in effect to continue as before. Smokers often get discouraged and despair of change. They make an effort, fail, and then confirm themselves with a self-diagnosis, "Compulsive smoker... incurable." These learned limitations can be bypassed by the unconscious mind. This applies to other habits as well.

One of our clients wanted to quit smoking and came for several sessions of hypnosis. We encouraged him to relax and be open to the creative potential of his trance experience. We sensed that he could make new, surprising discoveries before the next session, and suggested that he have some fun with it. He arrived at the next session smiling. He reported that he had a surprisingly wonderful time going out dancing with a girl the night before the session. He had gone to a disco and danced so well that everyone clapped. He told us with much embarrassment that he did not know how to dance nor did he usually go out with girls, since he was comfortably adjusted in a gay lifestyle. Some months later he got in touch to tell us that not only did he continue not smoking, but he had also continued dancing. He entered professional dance contests and was winning them! Furthermore, he discovered that he had ability as an excellent gourmet cook. His hidden natural talent evolved, freed from the restriction of rigid habit. He developed in new, unexpected, and positive directions, from his creative experiences opened up for him through trance.

Readying Unconsciously

Take your time. Go into a very deep trance. Relax and use any approach to trance you find effective. Deepen your trance several times, relax more with each suggestion, until you are deeper than you have ever been. Remember, levels vary with individuals and your unconscious will help you find an adequate depth for you.

Can you experimentally produce several different hypnotic effects? Try lightness, warmth, or heaviness of a limb with a nice image, or slowed experience of time, whatever you enjoy doing in trance. You know that you have begun to set yourself to give up smoking. But perhaps you will discover something positive and new to replace it. Experiment with altering your awareness, and be open to the unknown.

Have you ever lit a cigarette, set it down in an ashtray, and let it go out, forgotten? Or thought you still had a pack of cigarettes left, only to realize that none remained? Each exercise you do in trance can help enlist your unconscious in quitting. Just as your hand can sometimes move seemingly by itself when you write, or you sometimes feel too lazy to do anything, so also you can find the craving you usually feel for cigarettes can dissipate or be altered. New perceptions of smoking can arise from a different image in trance. This can help you change. A new insight about smoking may follow, or you may just stop without insight. Trust your unconscious to individualize.

Unconscious Strength

Explore your reactions to positive suggestions: can you imagine giving up cigarettes with little or no discomfort? Your body knows how to not notice many experiences and sensations. Unconscious wisdom can give inner involuntary strength, adding to conscious conviction. You find a new reservoir of confidence to help you. The discovery of your own untapped inner strength becomes the source of change.

You can be calm, using hypnosis when needed, if you are willing to use your unconscious to help. Your urge to smoke need not lead to actually smoking. At any point in the chain of action, a link can be broken. Then the habit loses its expression in action.

Associations and Imaginings

Imagine how you would be without your habit. What a positive sense of accomplishment you will have achieved! You may wonder why you did not change it sooner. What thoughts and images do you have as you project yourself into the future? How did you do it? What are you like? Your thoughts and associations flow from the source of change, but the source is not conscious. Let your unconscious help you in positive ways. Then relax and rest in trance. Wake up refreshed. Repeat this trance often over the next several days. You might want to emphasize suggestion of one aspect over another at each session. Some will find results are immediate, while others may need several sessions. Use trance in the ways that help you.

⌘

The relationship between yourself and your unconscious can grow and develop in beneficial ways if you work on it. As the river flows to the ocean and becomes one with it, your sincere intention to resolve your problems can lead you to open up better communication between your conscious and unconscious. People have many hidden unrecognized potentials, often kept in reserve unknowingly. Use hypnosis to cultivate receptivity to your hidden potential, so you can incorporate your own unrecognized resources into your life. We hope you can apply these learnings to accomplish your goals and beyond. As you change your habits, you may have a pleasant surprise. Potential can develop in other areas than just the target area. Everything you have experienced and learned can be a resource for positive change. But that is an even greater learning. Learning is infinite.

Fourteen

Stress Less

Calm, activity--each has its use.

--Zen Master Shaku Soen

L ife makes demands on us every day to meet challenges, adapt, and satisfy our needs as well as those of others we care about. These challenges, combined with striving to achieve, can induce stress. Stress has been researched for many years. Generally, findings show people can do something about how stress affects them. Some attitudes are better for withstanding stress. Relaxation skills clearly help; consequently hypnosis has been one of the treatments of choice for stress management.

Early Concepts of Stress

The word "stress" derives from the Middle English word *stresse*, meaning hardship. The Old French word *destresse* referred to constraint. Physics brought the word into the scientific arena in the 1700s, defining it as the force or pressure exerted on a material object. Over the centuries, physicists narrowed the definition to a very specific principle of elasticity, with its own equation.

Gradually the idea of stress found its way back to the realm of human experience. Sir William Osler, the famous early twentieth century physician, equated stress and strain with hard

233

work and worry. He said that every physician he knew suffered from it because of "the incessant treadmill of the practice of medicine, and in every one of these men there was an added factor--worry" (Hinkle 1973, 30).

Selye's General Adaptation Syndrome

Canadian physiologist Hans Selye (1907-) popularized the concept of stress as a distinct syndrome. He came up with this idea somewhat by accident. As a student in 1926, Seyle noticed all of the patients with different diseases shown to the medical students also seemed to share symptoms of a universal reaction to disturbance of homeostasis, such as tiredness and loss of appetite. At the time, Selye just conceptualized it as "being sick." He wondered if it was something more. It was not until the 1950s that Selye's research led him back to the implications of his early observations of a characteristic nonspecific reaction pattern. Whenever there is a continuous environmental stressor, he observed, the organism responds with this pattern. He called this reaction the General Adaptation Syndrome.

The General Adaptation Syndrome has three stages. First is the alarm reaction when internal resources are mobilized in an attempt to return the body to its normal balanced functioning, homeostasis. Second is the resistance, when the individual uses whatever resources available to fight off the effects of stress. If the stressor persists, the resources become depleted and the organism is exhausted for stage three. Seyle believed that these three stages occur in any stress situation. This syndrome is a nonspecific reaction of the body as it adjusts to demands that are placed upon it, returning to balance. This view is still widely accepted today.

Coping with Stress

Harold G. Wolff, a contemporary of Selye, developed the concept of "life stress." He believed stress was the result of people's interaction with harmful agents or circumstances. How people cope with these stressful elements can have a profound effect on how stress affects them. Barbara Snell Dohrenwend and Bruce P. Dohrenwend (1981) noted in their extensive research that some people become ill when exposed to life stress but others do not. They wondered why. They discovered cognitive processes play a large part in how stress affects people. Expectations about the stressfulness of an event can influence the effects of stress. People cope better when a situation is appraised as a challenge rather than a threat.

Irving Janis (1971) found coping well is due to accurate perception, expectation and preparation. He followed the outcome of patients undergoing major surgery and found that patients coped well when they had realistic expectations. Those who were properly informed had realistic expectations, were prepared well and therefore coped better, lessening the potentially harmful effects of postoperative stress. Those with unrealistically high expectations were disappointed and tended to be upset from the inevitable discomfort during recovery. A moderate amount of anxiety about potentially stressful events leads to adequate preparation for challenges and less difficulty subsequently coping or adjusting.

Richard Lazarus pointed out that cognitive appraisals, that is, how people interpret situations, can have an effect on coping with stress (Lazarus 1991, 14). Adaptation to stress includes the interpretation (both conscious and unconscious) of the events or stimuli. He believes how well people cope depends on how they appraise their circumstances and ability to manage them.

Lazarus distinguished between problem-focused coping and emotional-focused coping. (Lazarus, 1984, 1991) Stressors vary greatly, and require different coping strategies. For example, stress from your car not working when you need it is best managed by problem-focused coping. The death of a significant relative requires an emotionally focused coping strategy. Successful coping strategies can modify whether the situation or stimulus becomes helpful or harmful to the individual. (Lazarus, in Lipowski, Lipsitt, & Whygrow, 1977, 23)

Personality factors can also affect how stress is endured, whether it is experienced as an overwhelming threat or as a challenging opportunity. According to Suzanne Kobasa (1979) a personality trait gives the ability to endure stress by finding meaning and challenge in difficult life situations. She called this personality trait "hardiness."

Theorists have studied and correlated stressful changes in the social environment with illness. Hinkle (1967) reported increases in respiratory illness at crucial stressful points in a person's life. Smale (in Frank, 1973) found that serious illness often follows separation of some kind. Supportive therapeutic interaction can help in coping with such life events, enhancing a positive, hopeful response. Support may come from family, intimate relationships, friends, or co-workers. All of us have been reassured and helped at times by others during trying circumstances. As a result we felt much more comfortable. This is one of the values of supportive counseling interactions. According to research, this kind of help stimulates feelings of hope, raising morale. (Frank, 1973)

Hypnosis can encourage positive feelings and raise morale for contending with or enduring inevitable stress.

Good Stress Vs Bad Stress

Not all stress is bad for the organism. Researchers have found that sometimes stress seems to be positive, spurring an individual on to even better performance. For another individual, the same circumstances can be experienced as negative, resulting in a breakdown into illness or emotional discomfort.

Paradoxically, some illnesses are cured by stress (Whitehorn 1956). For example, victims exposed to trauma during World War II sometimes had surprising recoveries. Some soldiers and concentration camp survivors lost illnesses such as ulcers, migraines, and colitis, diseases that had previously been thought to be caused by stress. Others developed these problems.

Another surprising finding is pleasant circumstances can also bring about stress. People feel just as much stress when experiencing pleasure, *eustress*, as experiencing displeasure, *distress* (Selye, 1974). In both situations, stress is produced because the inner balance is disturbed. Either negative or positive experiences can be stressors when people continue to push themselves without rest. Eventually, hard-driving, hard-playing people may suffer secondary difficulty from stress-related diseases such as ulcers, back pain, high blood pressure and so on. Both positive excitement and negative tensions push us away from center. Restoring equilibrium is primary for healthy living. We need balance.

Modern researchers have found that people need a certain amount of manageable stress for optimum functioning. Whitehorn often said that people need challenge for growth and development. (Whitehorn 1956, 646). Without the challenge and meaningful involvement of "purposeful personal striving" (Whitehorn 1956, 647), people become unhappy and often ill. All stress is not to be avoided; sometimes it should be embraced. Manageable stress helps. Unmanageable stress harms.

Based upon the research that has been done on stress, you can learn to cope better. If your life presents you with difficult situations, you can withstand them better, with less harmful effects, activating and using your natural mechanisms You can use self hypnosis to achieve inner balance while functioning at your best.

Relaxation

One way of enduring stress is appropriate relaxation. You can learn to relax using hypnosis and then call upon this skill when you need it. The exercises that follow will help to develop a relaxed body and mind which has more general nonspecific effects. Use these and any other relaxation exercises presented throughout this book.

Body Relaxation Exercise

Find a comfortable position, either sitting or lying down. Close your eyes and allow your breathing to be relaxed. Suggest that as you drift into trance you can become more and more relaxed. Suggest that you can let go of any unnecessary tensions. As you feel ready, suggest that your relaxation can deepen. Rest comfortably for fifteen minutes or so, allowing yourself to remain very relaxed in trance. When you feel ready to return to full awareness, count backwards from five to one, suggesting that you will become more alert and refreshed with each number until you are fully awake and aware. Relax as often as possible during times of stress. A few minutes spent relaxing consistently morning and night helps to counterbalance the effects of potential stressors in your circumstances.

Some of our assumptions are conscious, and we can correct them rationally. Others are unconscious, and people simply behave accordingly, without quite recognizing that their behavior has its basis in unconscious assumptions. (Chapter 3) Hypnosis can influence your thinking patterns so you develop more healthy attitudes, both conscious and unconscious.

Conscious Observation

Ready yourself for trance, but before you actually go into trance, think about your concern. Consider what you feel and think about it. For example, if you are facing an exam, do you feel pessimistic? If your concern is work related, do you believe you have been unfairly burdened? Whatever the nature of your situation, try to become aware of your deeper attitudes.

Creative Problem Solving and Stress

Review some of the creative problem solving techniques in Chapter 7. Ask your unconscious if it can make some new discoveries. Are there other ways to think about your situation? Consider new possibilities. But do not try to impose them.

Unconscious Attitude Change

Now, go into trance. Allow your thoughts to drift, without directing them one way or the other. Simply remain curious what potential understandings your unconscious will discover within your situation. Remain in trance until you feel ready to wake up, refreshed and alert. Repeat this exercise over a period of time. Change of attitude may be subtle and slow at first, but keep inviting your unconscious to work on it. Change should be based in what can be, not what cannot be: a better understanding will follow.

Dissociation

Sometimes detachment gives the capacity to face with dignity what must inevitably be. You can use your ability to dissociate hypnotically for improved coping with difficult situations.

Trance Dissociation Skills

Sit in a chair with your hands resting on your knees. Relax as you go into trance. Let yourself experience sensations in your hands, as you have in previous exercises. As you relax even more deeply, can you experience your hands as being far away? Or perhaps your unconscious mind would like to give you this experience with your foot. Wait for your response. Observe as if watching from a distance.

Dissociating from Stress

Close your eyes. Sit comfortably in one of the usual positions. Let yourself go deeply into trance. Think of a time when you were not feeling under pressure. Perhaps

240

you were on vacation, or maybe you were having a lighter workload. Or if you are suffering from a prolonged illness, think back to a pleasant time before. Vividly recall how you felt. Bring to mind any memories associated with that time in your life. As you think about this, allow your body to relax naturally. Your thoughts may become calmer. When ready, awaken relaxed and refreshed.

Reclaiming Time

People often feel that they do not have enough time. We are goal-oriented, filling every minute with plans and activities. Internal conversations echo, "I have to go here; I've got to do that." Plans and goals are important and useful, but allowing some unplanned time to simply let be, can help return the busy person to balance. This ancient fable illustrates the point:

God sent an angel to earth to offer eternal life in exchange for a moment of human time. But the angel had to return to God without delivering the gift because, when he reached earth, he discovered that everyone was living with one foot in the past and one foot in the future. No one had a moment of time (Keene 1979, 70).

Hypnosis draws on the inner recesses of the mind, a timeless space of experience that does not rely on the ticking of a clock. Return to the time distortion exercises in Chapter 6. You can use this ability now to help in the midst of tough times. The ability of your inner mind to experience time in creative ways will allow a short trance to have long-lasting effects. This exercise can be done almost anytime: at your desk at the office, in the evening just before sleep, during your child's nap, or as part of your coffee break. Making this exercise, or any of the exercises included in this book, part of your daily routine can set the stage for a less harried, calmer but productive life.

Hypnotic Time Distortion Exercise

Take note of the time when you begin. Find a comfortable position, either seated or lying down. Close your eyes. Develop a deep, comfortable trance. Let go of any unnecessary tension. Imagine a favorite movie or book. Let yourself recall the story, from beginning to end. Imagine that you have all the time you need to review it. As you do so, enjoy the experience, feeling relaxed and entertained. When you have finished the entire story, wake up and check the time. You may feel as if a long time has elapsed, and yet, on the clock, only a few minutes have passed. Take some time here and there during your routines for this. You will then be able to return to your efforts with renewed energy.

Sometimes hypnosis can help you to literally work faster, thereby allowing you to accomplish tasks more quickly. Finishing earlier than expected can be a great stress reliever. During graduate school, one of the authors had a paper due at a certain time on a certain day. Finally the paper was written, but still needed to be typed. Unfortunately, there was not enough time to type the paper, given her usual typing speed. She decided to use hypnosis, went into trance and suggested that if her unconscious could find a way, she would type more quickly. Upon awakening, she began to type. Much to her surprise, the hands of the clock seemed to be moving more slowly as she typed at what felt like her usual speed. The paper was finished, but the clock seemed to indicate that plenty of time remained to get to school and turn in the paper. What she subsequently discovered was that her typing speed had increased markedly. This increase in typing speed remained part of her repertoir ever since, a useful enhancement of skill.

You can experiment with this for yourself. Practice some of the time distortion exercises in Chapter 6. Then try this exercise. Hypnosis is not magic, but you might be surprised how much latitude you have in accomplishing your tasks.

Working More Quickly

As you are beginning to drift into trance, suggest that you would like to find a creative way to accomplish a certain task more efficiently and quickly. You do not need to make exact specific descriptive suggestions. Instead, invite your unconscious to find a way, perhaps a very unique creative way, to work rapidly. Hold your attention on the task and allow your attention to drift around it, wondering what your creative way will be. Then, when you are ready, go even more deeply into trance. Remain in trance until you feel ready to return to your normal, waking state.

Happiness and Well Being

You can discover happiness and well being within, so that your life flows more smoothly. When you meet your circumstances with trust and confidence in your resources, you will feel better, and may master the challenges. Use this trance exercise to help you discover your own calm, confident center within, from your unconscious reservoir of potential, to help you enjoy well being and happiness. If you cannot seem to feel positive after a reasonable time, turn to the resistance chapter.

Positive Unconscious

Go deeply into trance, allowing your breathing rate to become comfortable, your muscles to relax, and a pleasant feeling to envelop you. Some feel a comfortable warmth, others might feel a refreshing coolness, or maybe lightness, heaviness, etc. Allow yourself to have your own response. Your unconscious response can be a positive ally in your life. You have felt confident in the past, at times. You did not do anything to make yourself feel confident, it just happened. Trust your response, permitting the time necessary. You have an untapped resource, that you can be in tune with.. As you relax even more, you can begin to feel your own deep calmness pervade your experiencing. This calmness will lead to a feeling of being centered and balanced. Let these feelings develop. Stay with this until you are ready to awaken, refreshed, with a feeling of well-being. Allow this experience to stay with you as long as you like.

⌘

Life's challenges await us
Though we cannot control our fate
We will meet contingency hopefully
As we step through destiny's gate.

--C. Alexander Simpkins

Bibliography

Bakan, P. "Hypnotizability, Laterality of Eye Movements and Functional Brain Asymmetry," *Perceptual and Motor Skills.* 28 1969: 927-32

Bandler, Richard. and John Grinder. *Patterns of the Hypnotic Techniques Milton H. Erickson, Vol.1.* Cupertino, California: Meta, 1975.

_____. *The Structure of Magic, Vol.1.* Palo Alto, California: Science & Behavior Books, 1975.

_____. *The Structure of Magic, Vol.2.* Palo Alto, California: Science & Behavior Books, 1976.

_____. *Trance Formations: Neurolinguistic Programming and the Structure of Hypnosis.* Moab, Utah: Real People Press, 1981.

Barber, Theodore X. "Hypnosis, Suggestions, and Psychosomatic Phenomena: A New Look From the Standpoint of Recent Experimental Studies." *American Society of Clinical Hypnosis,* Vol.21, No.1, July, 1978.

_____. N. Spanos, and J. Chaves, *Hypnosis, Imagination and Human Potentialities.* New York: Pergamon, 1974.

Bassin, R. "Consciousness and the Unconscious." A *Handbook of Contemporary Soviet Psychology.* Ed. M. Cole and I. Maltzman. New York: Basic Books, 1969.

Bateson, Gregory. *Steps to an Ecology of Mind.* New York: Ballantine Books, 1972.

Baudouin, Charles. *Suggestion and Autosuggestion.* New York: Bodd, Mead, and Co., 1921.

Beahrs, John O. *Unity and Multiplicity: Multi-level Consciousness of Self in Hypnosis., Psychiatric Disorder and Mental*

Health. New York: Brunner-Mazel, 1982.

Bellak, Leopold. & L. Small. *Emergency Psychotherapy and Brief Psychotherapy*. New York: Grune & Stratton, Inc., 1965.

Benson, Herbert. *The Relaxation Response*. New York: Avon Press, 1975.

_____. *The Mind/Body Effect*. New York: Simon & Schuster, 1979.

Berne, Eric. *Intuition and Ego States*. San Francisco: TA Press, 1977.

Bernheim, Hippelyte. *Hypnosis and Suggestion in Psychotherapy*. New York: Jason Aronson, 1973.

Binet, Alfred, and Charles Feré. *Animal Magnetism*. New York: D. Appleton, 1888.

Blakeslee, T. R. *The Right Brain*. New York: Berkley Press, 1983.

Bogen, J. "The Other Side of the Brain: An Appositional Mind." *The Nature of Human Consciousness*. Ed. R. Ornstein. San Francisco: W.W. Freeman, 1973.

Boring, Edwin. *A History of Experimental Psychology*. Englewood Cliffs, N.J.: Prentice Hall, 1950.

Braid, James. *Braid on Hypnotism*. New York: Julian Press, 1960.

Bramwell, J. Milne. *Hypnotism, Its History, Practice, and Theory*. London: Grant Richards. 1903.

Breuer, Josef, and Sigmund. Freud. *Studies on Hysteria*. New York: Basic Books, 1957.

Brooks, C. Harry. *The Practice of Autosuggestion by the Method of Emile Couéé*. Albuquerque, New Mexico: Sun Books, 1981.

Brooks, Charles V.W., *Sensory Awareness*. Santa Barbara, California: Ross-Erickson Pub., 1982

Bruno, Frank. *Think Yourself Thin*. New York: Barnes & Noble, 1972.

Burke, Kenneth. *A Rhetoric of Motives*. Berkeley, California: University of California Press, 1969.

Cannon, William B. *The Wisdom of the Body*. New York: W.W. Norton, 1963.

Carroll, John B., ed. *Language, Thought, and Reality: Selected Writings of Benjamin Lee Whorf*. Cambridge, Massachusetts: The M.I.T. Press, 1956.

Cheek, David. "Unconscious Perception of Meaningful Sounds during Surgical Anaesthesia as Revealed Under Hypnosis." *American Journal of Clinical Hypnosis,* 1, 101-113, 1959.

_____. "Awareness of Meaningful Sounds Under Anaesthesia: Considerations and a Review of the Literature." *Theoretical and Clinical Aspects of Hypnosis*. Symposium Specialists, Miami, Florida, 1979.

Clark, R. "Effect of Mental Practice on the Development of a Certain Motor Skill." *The Research Quarterly*. Vol. 31, No. 4, 1960.

Cooper, Linn F., and Milton H. Erickson. *Time Distortion in Hypnosis*: *An Experimental and Clinical Investigation*. New York: Irvington, 1982.

Coué, Emile. *How to Practice Suggestion and Autosuggestion*. New York: American Library Service, 1923.

Crutchfield, R.S. and D. Krech. *Theory and Problems of Social Psychology*. New York: McGraw-Hill, 1948.

Darnton, Robert. *Mesmerism*. New York: Shocken Books, 1970.

DeBono, Edward. *Lateral Thinking*. New York: Harper Colophon Books, 1973.

BIBLIOGRAPHY

_____. *Teaching Thinking*. London: Temple Smith, 1976.

Diamond, M.J. "Issues and Methods for Modifying Responsivity to Hypnosis." in *Annals of the New York Academy of Sciences*. New York: 1974: 296, 119-128.

Dohrenwend, Bruce P. and Barbara S. Dohrenwend. *Stressful Life Events and Their Concepts*. Brunswick, New Jersey: Rutgers University Press, 1981.

Dorcus, Roy. M. *Hypnosis and Its Therapeutic Applications*. New York: McGraw Hill, 1956.

_____. and Shaffer, Wilson G., *Textbook of Abnormal Psychology* Baltimore, Maryland: Williams and Wilkins Co., 1945

Erickson, Milton H. "Further Techniques of Hypnosis: Utilization Techniques." *American Journal of Clinical Hypnosis,* 2, 1959: 3-21.

_____. "Initial Experiments Investigating the Nature of Hypnosis." *American Journal of Clinical Hypnosis,* 7, 1964: 152-62.

_____. *Mind-Body Communications in Hypnosis*. New York: Irvington, 1986.

_____. and Rossi, E. *Hypnotherapy*. New York: Irvington, 1979.

_____. _____. and Rossi, S. *Hypnotic Realities*. New York: Irvington, 1976.

_____. and ____. *The Collected Papers of Milton H. Erickson*. 4 Vols. New York: Irvington, 1980.

_____. and ____. *Experiencing Hypnosis: Therapeutic Approaches to Altered States*. New York: Irvington, 1981.

Fisher, Seymour. *Body Experience in Fantasy & Behavior*. New York: Appleton-Century-Crofts, 1970

Frank, Jerome D. *Persuasion and Healing*. New York: Shocken

Books, 1973.

_____. *Psychotherapy and the Human Predicament*. New York: Shocken Books, 1978.

_____. and Frank, Julia B. *Persuasion and Healing*. Baltimore, Maryland: The Johns Hopkins University Press, 1991.

_____. Hoehn-Saric, R., and Gurland, B. "Focused Attitude Change in Neurotic Patients." *Journal of Nervous and Mental Disease*. 147, no.2, 1968: 124-33.

_____. et al "Attitude Change and Attribution of Arousal in Psychotherapy," *Effective Ingredients of Successful Psychotherapy*. New York: Brunner/Mazel, 1978.

_____. et al *Effective Ingredients of Successful Psychotherapy*. New York: Brunner/Mazel, 1978.

_____. "Mind-Body Relationships in Illness and Healing." *Journal of the International Academy of Precentive Medicine*, Vol. II. No. 3, 1975.

_____. "The Role of Hope in Psychotherapy." *International Journal of Psychiatry*. Vol. 5, No. 5, May, 1968.

_____. "The Faith that Heals." Commencement Address at the Johns Hopkins University School of Medicine., May 23, 1975.

_____. "Psychotherapy--The Transformation of Meanings: Discussion Paper." *Journal of the Royal Society of Medicine*. Vol. 79, June 1986.

Gardner, Howard. *The Shattered Mind*. New York: Vintage Books, 1974.

Gazzaniga, Michael S.. "The Split Brain in Man." *In the Nature of Human Consciousness*. Ed. R. Ornstein. San Francisco: W.H. Freeman, 1973.

_____. and LeDoux, J.E. *The Integrated Mind*. New York:

Plenum Press, 1978.

Gould, Heywood. *Headaches: Causes, Treatment, and Prevention.* New York: Barnes & Noble Books, 1973.

Gurwitsch, Aron. *Studies in Phenomenology and Psychology.* Evanston, Illinois: Northwestern U. Press, 1966.

Guthrie, Edwin. R. *The Psychology of Human Conflict.* New York: Harper, 1935.

Hadas, Moses. ed. *Essential Works of Stoicism.* New York: Bantam Books, 1961.

Haley, Jay *Strategies of Psychotherapy.* New York: Grune & Stratton, 1967b.

_____. *Conversations with Milton H. Erickson.* Vol.1 New York: W.W. Norton, 1985.

_____. *Advanced Techniques of Hypnosis and Therapy: Selected Papers of Milton H. Erickson, M.D.* New York: Grune & Stratton, 1967.

_____. *Uncommon Therapy.* New York: W.W. Norton, 1973.

Herrigel, Eugen. *Zen in the Art of Archery.* New York: Vintage Books, 1971.

Hilgard, Ernest R. *Hypnotic Susceptibility.* New York: Harcourt Brace Jovanovich, 1968.

_____. *Divided Consciousness: Multiple Controls in Human Thought and Action.* New York: John Wiley & Sons, 1977.

_____,and Josephine R. Hilgard, *Hypnosis in the Relief of Pain.* Los Altos, California: William Kaufman, 1975.

Hilgard, Josephine R. *Personality and Hypnosis: A Study of lmaginative Involvement.* Chicago, Illinois: University of Chicago Press, 1970.

Hinkle, L. E. "The Concept of Stress in the Biological and Social Sciences." *Science, Medicine, and Man* Vol.1, 1973, 31-48.

Hull, Clark. *Hypnosis and Suggestibility.* New York: Appleton, Century, Crofts, 1968.

Husserl, Edmund. *The Idea of Phenomenology.* The Hague: Martinus Nijhoff, 1964.

Jacobson, Edmund. *Progressive Relaxation:* Chicago, Illinois: University of Chicago Press, 1929.

James, William. *The Principles of Psychology.* Vol.1 & II. New York: Henry Holt & Co., 1896.

Janet, Pierre. *Psychological Healing,* Vol. I & II. New York: McMillan, 1925.

Janis, Irving. *Stress and Frustration.* New York: Harcourt Brace Javonovich, Inc., 1971.

Jourard, Sidney. *Disclosing Man to Himself.* New York: Van Nostrand, Reinhold, 1968.

_____. *The Transparent Self.* New York: Van Nostrand, Reinhold, 1971.

Jung, Carl G. *The Structure and Dynamics of the Psyche.* Vol.8. in the *Collected Works of C.G. Jung.* Princeton, New Jersey: Princeton University Press, 1981.

Keene, Betty. *Sensing, Letting Yourself Live.* San Francisco: Harper and Row, 1979.

Kimura, D. "The Asymmetry of the Human Brain." *Recent Progress in Perception.* Ed. R. Held and W. Richards. San Francisco: W.H. Freeman, 1976.

Kline, Milton V. *Freud and Hypnosis: The Interaction of Psychodynamics and Hypnosis.* New York: The Julian Press, 1958.

Kobasa, S. C. "Stressful Life Events, Personality, and Health: An Inquiry into Hardiness." *Journal of Personality and Social Psychology,* 42, 707-717.

Kroger, William S. *Clinical and Experimental Hypnosis.* Philadelphia, Pennsylvania: J.B. Lippincott, 1977.

Kubie, Lawrence. *Neurotic Distortion of the Creative Process.* New York: Noonday Press, 1975.

Lazarus, Richard S. *Emotion and Adaptation.* New York: Oxford University Press, 1991.

_____. and S. Folkman. *Stress, Appraisal, and Coping.* New York: Springer, 1984.

LeCron, Leslie. *Self Hypnotism: The Technique and its Use in Daily Living.* Englewood Cliffs, New Jersey: Prentice Hall, 1964.

Lipowski, Z.J., Lipsitt, Don R., Whybrow, Peter C. "Psychological Stress and Coping in Adaptaion and Illness," Richard S. Lazarus. *Psychosomatic Medicine.* New York: Oxford University Press, 1977.

Lozanov, Georgi. *Suggestology & Outlines of Suggestopedy,* New York: Gordon & Breach, 1977.

Luria, Alexander R. "The Brain and Conscious Experience." *British Journal of Philosophy,* 58, 1967: 467-76.

Maltz, Maxwell. *Psychocybernetics,* North Hollywood, California: Wilshire Book Co., 1960.

Marcel, Gabriel. *Mystery of Being.* Chicago, Illinois: Henry Reginery Co., 1969.

Miller, George A. "The Magical Number Seven, Plus or Minus Two: Some Limits on Our Capacity for Processing Information." *Psychological Review.,* 63, 81-97, 1956.

Montessori, Maria. *The Montessori Method by Maria Mon tessori,* New York: Schocken Books, 1964.

Munro, Henry S. *Handbook of Suggestive Therapeutics, Applied Hypnotism,* Psychic Science. St. Louis, Missouri: C.V.

Mosby Co., 1911.

Natadze, R.G. & Michael Cole. "Experimental Foundations of Uznadze's Theory of Set." *A Handbook of Contemporary Soviet Psychology,* New York: Basic Books, 1969.

Nebes, R. "Man's So-Called Minor Hemisphere." *The Human Brain.* Ed. M.C. Wittrock. Englewood Cliffs, New Jersey: Prentice-Hall, 1977.

Orne, Martin. "A Note on the Occurrences of Hypnosis Without Conscious Content." *International Journal of Clinical and Experimental Hypnosis.* Vol. XII, No.2, April, 1964.

Osborn, Alexander F. *Applied Imagination, Principles and Procedures of Creative Thinking.* New York: Charles Scribner's Sons, 1953.

Overstreet, Harry A. *About Ourselves.* Great Britain: Butler & Tanner, 1938.

Owen, George. *Hysteria, Hypnosis, & Healing: The Work of J. M. Charcot.* London: Dennis Dobson, 1971.

Pavlov, Ivan P. *Conditioned Reflexes: An Investigation of the Physiological Activity of the Cerebral Cortex.* New York: Dover, 1960.

Perls, Frederick. *Gestalt Therapy Verbatim.* Lafayette, California: Real People Press, 1969a.

_____. *Ego, Hunger, and Aggression.* New York: Vintage Books, 1969b.

_____. Ralph Hefferline, and Paul Goodman. *Gestalt Therapy,* New York: Dell Publishers, 1951.

Platinov, K. *The Word as a Physiological and Therapeutic Factor.* Moscow: Foreign Languages Publishing House, 1959.

Prince, Morton. *Psychotherapeutics.* Boston: The Gorham Press,

1912.

Pulos, L. "Mesmerism Revisited: The Effectiveness of Esdaile's Techniques in the Production of Deep Hypnosis and Total Body Hypnoanaesthesia," *American Journal of Clinical Hypnosis,* Vol.22, No.4, Apr1980, 206-211.

Raudsepp, Eugene. *Creative Growth Games.* New York: Jove, 1977.

_____. *More Creative Growth Games.* New York: G.P. Putnam's Sons, 1980.

Reik, Theodore. *Listening With the Third Ear.* New York: Jove Publications, Inc., 1948.

Richardson, A. "Mental Practice: A Review and Discussion, Part I." *The Research Quarterly,* Vol. 38, No. 1, 1967.

_____. "Mental Practice, A Review and Discussion, Part II. *The Research Quarterly.* Vol. 38, No. 2, 1967.

Rosen, Sidney. *My Voice Will Go With You: The Teaching Tales of Milton H. Erickson.* New York: W.W. Norton, 1982.

Rossi, Ernest L. *Dreams and Growth of Personality.* New York: Pergamon Press, 1972.

_____. *The Psychobiology of Mind-Body Healing,* New York: W.W. Norton, 1986.

_____. "The Cerebral Hemispheres in Analytic Psychology." *Journal ofAnalytic Psychology,* 22, 1977: 32-51.

_____. "The Breakout Heuristic," *Journal of Humanistic Psychology,* 1968, Vol.8, 16-28.

_____."Hypnosis and Ultradian Cycles: A New State Theory of Hypnosis." *American Journal of Clinical Hypnosis,* 25, No.1, 1982: 21-31.

_____. Cheek, D. B. *Mind Body Therapy,* New York: W.W. Norton, 1988.

Sarbin, Theodore R. "Contributions to Role-Taking Theory." *Hypnotic Behavior. Psychological Review.* 5, 1950: 255-290.

Schmideberg, Miletta. "The Role of Suggestion in Analytic Therapy." *Psychoanalytic Review.* 26, 1939: 219-226.

Seyle, Hans. *Stress Without Distress.* New York: Signet Books, 1974.

Shaffer, G. Wilson. and Lazarus, R.S. *Fundamental Concepts in Clinical Psychology.* New York: McGraw-Hill, 1952.

Sidis, Boris. *The Psychology of Suggestion.* New York: D. Appleton, 1898.

Simpkins, C. Alexander & Annellen M. Simpkins. *Principles of Meditation: Eastern Wisdom for the Western Mind.* Boston: Charles E. Tuttle Co., Inc., 1996.

_____. & _____. *Living Meditation: From Principle to Practice.* Boston: Charles E. Tuttle Co., Inc. 1997a.

_____. & _____. *Zen Around the World.* Boston: Charles E. Tuttle Co., Inc., 1997b.

_____. & _____. *Meditation From Thought to Action..* Boston: Charles E. Tuttle Co., Inc., 1998.

_____. & _____. *Simple Zen: A Guide to Living Moment by Moment.* Boston: Charles E. Tuttle Co., Inc., 1999.

_____. & _____. *Simple Taoism: A Guide to Living in Balance.* Boston: Charles E. Tuttle Co., Inc., 1999.

_____. & _____. *An Outcome Comparison between Indirect Hypnotherapy and Insight Psychotherapy with Consideration Given to Hemisphere Dominance Effect.* Doctoral Dissertation. United States International University, 1983.

Sluzki, Carlos and Donald C. Ransom, *Double Bind: The*

Foundation of the Communicational Approach to the Family. New York: Grune & Stratton, 1976.

Springer, Sally P. and Georg Deutsch,. *Left Brain, Right Brain*. San Francisco: W.H. Freeman, 1981.

Suzuki, Daisetz. T. *Zen and Japanese Culture*. Princeton, New Jersey: Princeton University Press, 1959.

Taylor, Eugene. *Willian James on Exceptional Mental States*, New York: Charles Scribner's & Sons, 1982

Thorndike, Edward. Lee. *Human Learning,* Cambridge, Massachusetts: M.I.T. Press, 1977.

Tinterow, Moritz M. *Foundations of Hypnosis, From Mesmer to Freud*. Springfield, Illinois: Charles C. Thomas, 1970.

Uznadze, Dmitrii Nikolaevich. *The Psychology of Set*. New York: Consultants Bureau, 1966.

Watts, Alan. *The Way of Zen*. New York: Vintage Books, 1957.

Watzlawick, Paul, John H. Weakland. and Richard. Fisch. *Change*. New York: W.W. Norton & Co., 1974

Weitzenhoffer, Andre. *General Techniques of Hypnotism*. New York: Grune & Stratton, 1957.

_____. *Hypnotism: An Objective Study in Suggestibility*. New York: John Wiley & Sons, 1953.

_____. *The Practice of Hypnotism,* Vol.1 & Vol.11: New York: John Wiley and Sons, 1989.

_____. "Hypnotic Susceptibility Revisited,"*American Journal of Clinical Hypnosis*. Vol.22, No.3, 1980: 130-146.

Whitehorn, John. "The Concept of Meaning and Cause in Psychodynamics." *American Journal of Psychiatry,* 104, 1944: 289.

_____. "Stress and Emotional Health," *The American Journal of Psychiatry,* Vol.112, No.10, Apr.1956.

_____. "The Person, the Situation, and the Reaction: Psycho-therapeutic Strategy." *Acta Medical Scaninavia* Supp., 196, 1947: 626-33.

Wolberg, Lewis. *Medical Hypnosis,* Vol.1 & II. New York: Grune & Stratton, 1948.

_____. *Hypnoanalysis.* New York: Grune & Stratton, 1964.

_____. *Techniques of Psychotherapy.* Vol. I & II. New York: Grune & Stratton, 1977.

Wolff, Harold. *Proceedings of the Association for Research in Nervous and Mental Disease,* Baltimore, Maryland: Williams & Wilkins, 1950.

Wolpe, Joseph. *The Practice of Behavior Therapy.* New York: Pergamon, 1990.

Zaner, Richard M. *The Way of Phenomenology.* New York: Pegasus, 1970.

Zeig, Jeffrey A. *Teaching Seminar with Milton H. Erickson.* New York: Brunner/Mazel, 1980.

_____. *Ericksonian Approaches to Hypnosis and Psychotherapy.* New York: Brunner Mazel, 1982.